"Wow...a beauty book by the gorgeous Nancy St[...] secrets would she share that could change my life? '[...] ing ourselves as God sees us.' Nancy reminds us th[...] defines our real beauty. Buy this book, apply it...bec[...] secret I know."

JENNI BORSELLINO, TELEVISION COHOST, *AT HOME LIVE WITH CHUCK AND JENNI*

"I was tremendously blessed by Nancy's willingness to honestly share her own painful struggles for self-identity and the freedom and growth she has found in relationship with God through His love."

MARILYN MCCOO, SINGER

"Nancy Stafford offers a perspective I wish I'd had growing up, and one I hope to pass on to my daughter.... Nancy, my glasses were purple."

CONNIE SELLECCA, ACTRESS

"With honesty, vulnerability, and passion, Nancy Stafford opens up her own beautiful life to encourage us that we are all truly beautiful and deeply loved by God. Now that I've finished the last page and wiped away my tears, I'm starting a list of all the women in my life to whom I must give this inspiring book. Thank you, Nancy!"

KAREN COVELL, TELEVISION PRODUCER AND COAUTHOR OF
*THE DAY I MET GOD AND HOW TO TALK ABOUT JESUS WITHOUT FREAKING OUT*

"Nancy's personal experiences reveal her secrets of true and lasting beauty. I commend her for a beautiful book. A must-read for all women who seek spiritual truth and enlightened love."

RHONDA FLEMING, AUTHOR AND HUMANITARIAN

"Getting to know Nancy Stafford personally has been one of the great blessings of my life. I invite all of you to experience the joy of her compassionate heart. It seems impossible that such an exquisitely beautiful woman has suffered deep wounds in her self-image, but here Nancy allows God to use her scars to take us all on a healing journey toward wholeness and freedom. Nancy's writing reaches down into the hidden crevices of the heart and allows God to heal the deep wounds of childhood long buried there. Through the pages of Nancy's inspiring book, God reached into my own heart and healed some old wounds I didn't even know I had! He will do it for you, too."

SUSAN WALES, AUTHOR OF *STANDING ON THE PROMISES*

"The search for acceptance can be a long and painful one. And for many women, the gap between outward appearances and the cry of their heart can be huge. Nancy's story builds a bridge connecting our inside and our outside. The result is the revelation of a beauty that will heal."

HENRY CLOUD, PH.D., AUTHOR OF
*CHANGES THAT HEAL* AND COAUTHOR OF THE BESTSELLING *BOUNDARIES*

"As a young girl, I used to love fairy tales. *Beauty by the Book* has all the elements of a contemporary fairy tale, but the beauty of this story is that it's reality, not fantasy! It is full of deep spiritual truths that mothers and daughters everywhere should experience together."

DEBBY BOONE, VOCALIST AND AUTHOR OF *BEDTIME HUGS FOR LITTLE ONES*

"Nancy Stafford is a beautiful woman—inside and out. She strikes a perfect balance between unmasking the lies that the world tells us about beauty and reaffirming the value of taking care of ourselves and being the best we can be. Nancy tackles this often-misunderstood subject with great heart, humor, and personal humility. Every woman will find herself somewhere in these pages. Beauty by the Book is a must-read for women of all ages."

MELODY GREEN, AUTHOR, SPEAKER, AND CONTEMPORARY CHRISTIAN SONGWRITER

"If only all women would embrace the amazing truths in *Beauty by the Book*! Nancy Stafford gives us food for thought, as well as clarifies the fact that our issues with beauty run deep. By unearthing God's concept of beauty, we see ourselves from another point of view…as fearfully and wonderfully crafted vessels to behold!"

BUNNY WILSON, AUTHOR OF *SEVEN SECRETS WOMEN WANT TO KNOW*

"Honest, transparent, and liberating, *Beauty by the Book* speaks gently to a woman's deepest heart's cry. Nancy Stafford sets the record straight: We are not the sum total of what we see in the mirror. She points us to the One who created beauty and challenges us to discover the true source of our identity. If you've ever struggled with your own external qualities, this book will force you to take another look at yourself—and to celebrate the fact that you were wonderfully created by divine design…inside and out."

MICHELLE MCKINNEY HAMMOND, AUTHOR OF
*IF MEN ARE LIKE BUSES, THEN HOW DO I CATCH ONE?*

"Nancy's ability to focus on true inner beauty in the midst of a culture that bombards us with beauty that's only 'skin deep' is completely refreshing. Her vulnerability in sharing her pains (even the ones that seem insignificant) and her healing is a beautiful reminder to us that Jesus not only heals us, but also bears our pain…and that through Him we can walk in the wholeness He has provided."

KIM HILL, CONTEMPORARY CHRISTIAN RECORDING ARTIST

"Nancy Stafford's *Beauty by the Book* is one of the most touching books I've read. It is a must-read for any woman—young or old, large or thin, tall or short—who has ever felt ugly, insecure, fat, invisible, unloved, or unwanted—and isn't that really all of us? If you wonder how you can ever be, or more importantly, feel beautiful, you have to read Nancy's book. It rips your heart out and draws tears from your eyes…and then leaves you feeling loved, accepted, and beautiful!"

VICTORYA MICHAELS ROGERS, FORMER HOLLYWOOD AGENT AND COAUTHOR OF
*THE DAY I MET GOD AND HOW TO TALK ABOUT JESUS WITHOUT FREAKING OUT*

# BEAUTY

### *by the*

# BOOK

## NANCY STAFFORD

Multnomah® Publishers *Sisters, Oregon*

BEAUTY BY THE BOOK
published by Multnomah Publishers, Inc.

© 2002 by Nancy Stafford
International Standard Book Number: 1-57673-950-3

Cover design by David Carlson Design
Cover image of rose by Photodisc
Cover photo by Russell Baer

Scripture quotations are from:
*The Holy Bible,* New International Version © 1973, 1984 by
International Bible Society, used by permission of Zondervan Publishing House
*The Living Bible* (TLB) © 1971. Used by permission of
Tyndale House Publishers, Inc. All rights reserved.
*The Message* © 1993 by Eugene H. Peterson
*Revised Standard Version Bible* (RSV) © 1946, 1952 by the
Division of Christian Education of the National Council of the Churches of Christ
in the United States of America
*The Amplified Bible* (AMP) © 1965, 1987 by Zondervan Publishing House.
*The Amplified New Testament* © 1958, 1987 by the Lockman Foundation.

*Multnomah* is a trademark of Multnomah Publishers, Inc.,
and is registered in the U.S. Patent and Trademark Office.
The colophon is a trademark of Multnomah Publishers, Inc.

Printed in the United States of America

For information:
MULTNOMAH PUBLISHERS, INC. • P.O. BOX 1720 • SISTERS, OR 97759

Library of Congress Cataloging-in-Publication Data:
Stafford, Nancy.
    Beauty by the book: seeing yourself as God sees you / by Nancy Stafford.
        p. cm.
Includes bibliographical references.
    ISBN 1-57673-950-3 (pbk.)
    1. Christian women—Religious life.              I. Title.
    BV4527 . S73 2001
    248.8'43—dc21

                                                        2001006365

03 04 05 06 07 08—10 9 8 7 6 5 4 3 2

# Table of Contents

# WITH GRATITUDE

Heartfelt thanks to my many friends for your prayers, encouragement, guidance, and, in the case of Henry Cloud, friendly coercion and policing my progress.

I am especially grateful to Gayle Miller, Judie Lawson, Julaine Calhoun, Apphia Merino, Matilda Novak, and Mary Main. Many thanks to Susan Wales for our power-prayer walks and for your generosity in introducing me to the great folks at Multnomah.

My deep thanks to Don Jacobson, Bill Jensen, Penny Whipps, and Dave and Heather Kopp for believing in me and my message.

Thank you to my wonderful editor—and new friend—Judith St. Pierre, for your vision, for your heart…and for your beauty.

# A TRUE MIRROR

THEY SAY TO WRITE what we know. This I know: Real beauty isn't what we see in magazines or on movie screens, and it doesn't depend on the opinions of others or the changing tastes of culture. True beauty is seeing ourselves as God sees us, reflected in the mirror of His Word.

Inner beauty—knowing who we really are—is the message closest to my heart because it's been a lifelong search and a long, hard journey to reach the point where I really *believe* and *feel* that I am worth something, that I have value, that I am beautiful.

Believe me, no one would have used the word *pretty* to describe me when I was growing up. Tallest in my class by a head and shoulders, I was a gangly, gawky, unattractive kid. I had Casper-white skin with freckles galore, buckteeth, and glasses as thick as Coke bottles. My scraggly, wispy pigtails started off in the right spot when I left for school but somehow always wound up front-to-back, cyclops-style, by the end of the day. You get the general idea.

I grew up in a wonderful, loving Christian home. I felt secure in my parents' love, and I fell in love with Christ when I was eight years old. Even as a little girl, I would feel God's intimate, tender love for me, and my tears would flow. God gave me a sensitive heart. I've always felt things very deeply. But I didn't understand then the flip side of feeling deeply. Yes, I was receptive to His Spirit and His presence, and that was wonderful. But I was also very sensitive—too sensitive—to the attitudes and comments of the people around me.

My family tried to reassure me. "Nancy, honey, you're so beautiful on the inside. That's what counts," Mom would say.

Yeah, right.

When I was in first grade, I was painfully shy and terribly insecure, so Mom enrolled me in a ballet class. I loved it! This was where I could shine! I would rush into class every Saturday and dance with abandon—twirling, spinning, and leaping on my spindly legs, feeling absolutely beautiful and totally confident in my little pink tutu.

The mothers would gather in the back of the class to pick up their ballerinas, and one Saturday I glanced back and saw that they were all looking at me. *They must like my dancing!* I thought. Then I overheard the teacher say, "Oh yes, the girls are all doing so beautifully...except for that little Stafford girl. She's the clumsiest, most awkward child I've ever seen." They all laughed uproariously.

I was stunned. Mortified. Tears burned in my eyes, and I hid my face in my tutu and ran across the room to bury myself in my mom's big, soft, pillowy chest. I think that was the day I realized that what I had suspected about myself was true: I wasn't worth much. I wasn't valuable. And I was ugly.

No matter what my dear family said or did to try to convince me otherwise, I didn't believe them. They were my family; they had to say that. That big world out there told me something else, and I believed it instead. That day a lie lodged in my six-year-old heart: *You're ugly. You're clumsy. We don't want you.* And that day I put up my first wall of protection. Through the years other walls followed, all to help ward off the pain, loneliness, and rejection of being different from others, not accepted, and not really understood.

"Nancy, honey, you're so beautiful on the inside. That's what counts," Mom would say.

Somehow I knew that it should have been true—that inner beauty *was* more important—but as I looked around, even at age six or seven or eight, I noticed that it didn't really count that much, at least not as far as how people treated you. The physically beautiful, the socially acceptable, and the currently fashionable were what people—even in the church—really accepted and esteemed. And that wasn't me. Goodness and kindness and consideration, the traits my family possessed and taught me were important, didn't seem to matter nearly as much as popularity, a sassy comeback, the right clothes, and a pretty face.

For many years I struggled to reconcile what God wanted me to be with what the world told me I should be—a struggle that continued even after I began modeling and acting.

For twenty years now I've enjoyed a wonderful career in television as an actress and as the host of an international fashion and beauty TV series. I've modeled in New York and been in the Miss America pageant. I know the tricks of the trade. But what I know most about beauty has nothing to do with my profession.

Quite the opposite.

What I know most about beauty has come from God healing my heart and showing me who I really am. He has turned the ashes of my life into beauty, the mourning into joy. He will do the same for you. He wants to love you into being!

That's what this book is about.

It isn't a "how-to" beauty book.

It isn't *Five Easy Steps to a New You.*

It's a book about freedom from the bondage of our culture's

unattainable standards, freedom from lies of the past that have told us who we are, and, yes, even freedom from the lie that outward appearance means nothing. It's a book about the beauty our spirits are drawn to because we have been made in the very image of Beauty Himself.

Everyone has beauty, but not everyone sees it. I want you to see it.

Each piece in this book begins with a promise about who you are in Christ. Through these promises, I want you to get a picture of who you really are—of who God says you are. I want you to look into the mirror of God's Word and see yourself as He sees you. I want you to know how much He loves you and how much you have because of His Son.

When you know who you really are, you glow with an inner radiance and confidence that affects every other part of your life. And as you absorb the truth of how much God loves you and grab hold of the promises He has made you, you'll be surprised and delighted as you see yourself being transformed into the vibrant, healthy, complete, beautiful woman you were always meant to be.

Maybe this isn't the kind of beauty book you expected. Perhaps it's more of a makeover book, one that offers rebirth and rejuvenation in those areas that need a little cleansing, some refreshing, and new life. That's the kind of beauty I care about—the real beauty that comes as we become everything God created us to be.

I'm writing this book because I want you to grasp the depth of God's love for you, to discover and embrace the beauty within you, and then to delight in the unique beauty He has reserved for you alone.

I'm writing this book because I want you to see the beauty of others, so that, free of envy and comparisons, you can encourage their beauty and help them flourish.

I'm writing this book because beauty has been a big part of my life. I've experienced both its pain and its promise. As a homely young girl, it eluded me. As a model in New York, it seduced me. As an actress in Hollywood, its importance distresses me. And as a woman who loves God, the power of true beauty staggers me.

Beauty. It's seldom what we think it is. True beauty is inner beauty—beauty by the Book.

I invite you to come with me as I share my life, my reflections, and my struggles on my own path to beauty. Join me on a journey from insecurities and fear, through brokenness and doubt, all the way to fullness and truth—all the way to knowing, beyond a shadow of a doubt, what the psalmist proclaimed: "The king is enthralled by your beauty" (Psalm 45:11).

*Beauty of form affects the mind,*
*but then it must not be the*
*mere shell that we admire,*
*but the thought that this shell is only the beautiful case*
*adjusted to the shape and value of a still*
*more beautiful pearl within.—Jane Porter*

# CHAPTER ONE

# BEAUTY MATTERS

# The Power of Appearances

He does not judge me by appearances...

*Stop judging by mere appearances,*
*and make a right judgment.—John 7:24*

THE HOTEL BALLROOM was jammed. It was the biggest fundraiser of the year for the American Red Cross. Everybody who was anybody was there. Philanthropists mixed with politicians mixed with Rotary Club. I was Miss Florida. I wore a red evening gown draped with a satin and velvet sash that said so.

*Ouch!* With every move of my head, one of the three-inch bobby pins keeping my crown aloft jabbed into my skull and pinched my teased scalp, bringing me to near tears. I imagined a handful of hair being yanked out at the roots. Surely I must be bleeding by now. Better check. Looking for an escape route to the ladies room to recrown myself, I saw...her. As Sherlock Holmes referred to the character of Irene Adler, she was...The Woman.

Tall, regal, elegant, graceful. Golden brown body and near platinum blond hair. Her ivory crepe evening gown stood out like a lighthouse in a sea of blinding rhinestones, bright chiffon...and pageant-sashed red. Proof of her refinement and elegance. She was compassionate too, I could tell. Probably a Red Cross volunteer *and* a philanthropist. She laughed easily but had a mysterious reserve.

Royalty, maybe? Sweden or Bulgaria, I guessed. Someplace far away. And elegant. I couldn't take my eyes off her. She was a vision. Did I say she was elegant? She was everything I wanted to be.

Then, unbelievably, I saw that she was looking at me. She gave a small, elegant smile. Wow. Warm feelings washed over me. This creature, this *vision* had noticed me! I felt as though she was inviting me into some inner circle. I glanced around. Nope, nobody else. Just me. Of all the hundreds of people in the whole room, she was looking at *me!* Then I felt the bobby pin jab. Oh yeah, I had a crown on my head. Who wouldn't notice?

It didn't matter; I had to meet her. I grasped the sleeve of my pageant chaperone, Donna Jean, and we slowly made our way across the room. To my amazement, The Woman had begun to walk toward me too, weaving her way through the crowd like an ivory ribbon.

We both began to speak at the same time. Laughing nervously, I deferred. After all, she was The Woman. She brushed a platinum wisp off her perfect face, smiled that elegant smile, and then, in an octave lower and a volume louder than I expected, said in a gravelly kind of rasp, "Ya know, I was Miss New Joisey once-st. Miss Casino, USA. Yeah! Woulda gone onta da nationals too, but dem blankity-blanks found out about me an one-a dem judges. Ah well, dat's da breaks. I just came ta dis ting wit Joey. *Hey, Joey!* Get me anudda drink!"

I was stunned. A bucket of cold water in the face would have been less startling. Hoping that my bulging eyes and slack jaw hadn't given me away, I managed, "Well…uh…I'm not the least bit surprised! You're…beau…tiful!"

*That which is striking and beautiful is not always good; but that which is good is always beautiful.* —Ninon do l'Enclos

How deceived we are by appearances! We exalt some people and dismiss others, sometimes at first glance, based on how they look to us. That's what I did. I supposed some things about "Miss New Joisey" and attributed certain qualities to her based purely on her appearance. At a glance, I made her the embodiment of beauty and grace, only to find that she was a flawed mortal just like the rest of us.

That evening shook me. Yes, I've laughed about it over the years as a "funny story," but its deeper truth haunts me. How many times have I dismissed people with true elegance and inner beauty just because of their packaging? Do I still blindly deify some, yet blithely disregard others? Even in a tiny way, am I prejudiced toward the attractive, while missing the true beauty of the seemingly plain ones in front of me? Truthfully now, what do I think deep down when I look at that ratty street person, that pencil-thin and fashionable neighbor, that grossly overweight woman, or that photogenic superstar? Even when we know better, we judge. We esteem and we disparage, we elevate and we denigrate—all based on appearance.

But even though we sometimes do, God is One who does not judge by mere appearances. And how grateful I am for that fact when I'm the one He is looking at.

*We live in a fantasy world, a world of illusion.*
*The great task in life is to find reality.—Iris Murdoch*

# Our Longing for Beauty

I will gaze upon the beauty of the Lord forever…

*One thing I ask of the Lord, this is what I seek: that I may dwell in the house of the Lord all the days of my life, to gaze upon the beauty of the Lord and to seek him in his temple.*—*Psalm 27:4*

THE TRUTH IS THAT WE *need* beauty in our lives. We were made in the very image of Beauty: Christ Himself. Our first home was a place unsurpassed in its natural beauty—perfect, in fact—Eden. We are born with a deep longing for and appreciation of beauty. Our spirits are drawn to it. It calls to us, nourishes us, stimulates us.

Think about how you feel when the beauty of nature surrounds you, how nourished, refreshed, whole. A shady forest trail, a sparkling sandy beach, a majestic thundering waterfall, a tiny fragrant garden— all have the power to renew us. We drink in their beauty; we savor it.

What happens to you when you see a powerful work of art or hear a stirring piece of music? Don't you feel nurtured and nourished when you walk into the elegant lobby of a great hotel or a tastefully decorated home, enjoy a deliciously magnificent meal, or meet a vibrant, confident person?

Beauty is a baby's toothless, dimpled smile that makes you grin from ear to ear. It's a fragrant bouquet and the mellow taste of a rich red wine rolling slowly in your mouth. Beauty is art that transfixes. Literature that transports. The violin cry that breaks your heart and moves you to tears. The driving drum that bores deep in your bones and inflames your soul.

Surrounded and awakened from slumber, my senses can hardly take it. *Stop!* I cry. Then, *No! Give me more.*

*What delights us in visible beauty is the invisible.*——*Marie von Ebner-Eschenbach*

At its most magnificent, though, earthly beauty is but a paltry taste, a dim foreshadow, of what awaits. C. S. Lewis reminds us that the beauty we are drawn to—nature or art or music or books—is not the ultimate, only the conduit:

> It was not in them, it only came through them, and what came through them was longing…. They are not the thing itself; they are only the scent of a flower we have not found, the echo of a tune we have not heard, news from a country we have never yet visited.[1]

What we yearn for is the beauty of heaven. Eternity has been set in our hearts, and it burns there in our secret longing. Lewis writes:

> In this universe…the longing to…bridge some chasm that yawns between us and reality is part of our inconsolable secret. And surely…the promise of glory…becomes highly relevant to our deep desire. For glory meant good report with God, acceptance by God, response, acknowledgment, and welcome into the heart of things. The door on which we have been knocking all our lives will open at last….

Apparently, then, our lifelong nostalgia, our longing to be reunited with something in the universe from which we now feel cut off, to be on the inside of some door which we have always seen from the outside, is no mere neurotic fancy, but the truest index of our real situation. And to be at last summoned inside would be both glory and honour beyond all our merits and also the healing of that old ache.[2]

One day our longing and ache will end. Our hunger will be satisfied. Our great heart-cry, the one thing we ask—to gaze upon the beauty of the Lord—will be answered. The door will open. And we shall be one with Him. Until then, we long for beauty and desperately need it in our lives.

*In all ranks of life the human heart yearns for the beautiful;*
*and the beautiful things that God makes*
*are his gift to all alike.——Harriet Beecher Stowe*

# THE IMPORTANCE OF BEAUTY

He crowns me with love and compassion...

*Praise the Lord, O my soul, and forget not all his benefits—who forgives all your sins and heals all your diseases, who redeems your life from the pit and crowns you with love and compassion.—Psalm 103:2–4*

A WOMAN'S APPEARANCE is an important part of her need for beauty. A woman can be interested in both blush and the boardroom, mascara and ministry, fashion and physics, hair gel and homeschooling, or working out and working with the homeless. One doesn't cancel out the other, and wanting to look good doesn't make you a shallow person or a self-consumed sinner.

We all know that how we look influences how we feel. Be honest: Don't you feel better at the post office when your hair looks good, you have on a dab of makeup, and you're dressed nicely? Isn't it better than waiting in line hoping that nobody sees you in your sloppy clothes, with your dirty hair bundled up in a ponytail? (Okay, okay! I admit it: That was me you saw in the express mail line!)

And have you noticed that when you feel better about yourself, you're more apt to smile and talk with others? Believe me, I wear makeup so much for work that I love the days I can run around in sweats or shorts and not have to do my face or hair. And I do. (You've seen me at the post office, remember?) But I also know that I feel better and more willing to engage with others when I'm confident about my appearance.

According to some psychologists, when you're looking after your appearance, you're also looking after your *self*—your emotional life, your self-esteem. It seems to follow that taking care of yourself automatically improves the way you see yourself. You respect yourself. And by caring for your appearance, you are telling the world that you are a person worthy of respect. The bottom line is that when you feel better about you, you're more confident, so you can forget about yourself for two seconds and focus on somebody else.

Psychologists are also becoming more aware of the link between making the effort to look good and feeling happy. They note that people who are depressed or emotionally fragile just don't think it's worth the effort to groom themselves. As one therapist told me: "When people are very depressed, their self-care is low. When we start to see grooming reemerge, we know they are improving. There's no doubt that both psychological and physical health demand that people pay attention to their needs."

I've seen firsthand the psychological and emotional benefits of improved appearance. When the beautiful actress Rhonda Fleming lost her sister to cancer, she determined to create a place of beauty, care, and compassion for women going through that nightmare. She established the Rhonda Fleming Center for Women with Cancer at UCLA Medical Center and filled it with warm colors, lovely furnishings, paintings…and love. Then she asked our mutual friend, Vera Brown, for help.

For thirty years, my dear friend Vera has been the facial, body care, and makeup maven to L.A.'s most beautiful people. But her favorite clients aren't film stars, cover girls, or socialites; they are women fresh out of chemotherapy.

Every week for many years, Vera joined Rhonda at the cancer center, giving these ladies what they needed to feel feminine and beautiful again. She brought wigs, creams, makeup…and hope. She rolled up her sleeves, dipped her hands, and soothed away the pain, fear, and loss that cancer causes. Her creams are legendary, but it was her touch that restored.

A dozen or more women would gather in a room, some just days after surgery or hours after chemo. Unhurriedly, Vera gave each woman a facial, did their makeup, and taught them how to have beautiful eyes—no lashes or brows required. And as she did, she told them: "Nothing comes out of a jar that does as much for you as your spiritual attitude. When you have that and love yourself, you're truly beautiful."

Vera is proud of the business she's built—the photo-lined walls, the magazine spreads, and the national awards—but true satisfaction lights up her beautiful face when she talks about "her girls." These women are proof of the psychological benefits of improved appearance for the self-esteem of cancer patients. Paying attention to the way they look has a huge therapeutic impact on them. Suddenly they realize that, no matter what has happened to them, their beauty is more than just the sum of their parts. They see that they are worthy of attention, and just knowing that makes it easier for them to cope. And as they adjust, they are better able to pour out on others the love and compassion that encourages their beauty and helps them flourish too.

Several years ago, Vera had to begin to practice what she preached: She woke up one morning to find a lump in her breast. And the women she had embraced, cared for, and comforted now surrounded her with love and support and affection.

*There is no beautifier of complexion, or form, or behavior, like the wish to scatter joy and not pain around us.—Virgil*

ℰ

# MERE APPEARANCES

He sees my heart...

*The Lord said to Samuel, "Do not consider his appearance or his height.... The Lord does not look at the things man looks at Man looks at the outward appearance, but the Lord looks at the heart." —1 Samuel 16:7–8*

I REMEMBER THE DAY I noticed my family was different. I think I was five.

I was with Mom and Dad and my older brother, Tracy. We were in a shopping mall. A young family nearby glanced our way, looked a little longer, and then began to snicker and stare. The father saw us first and elbowed his son. The two children pointed, giggled, and, to the amusement of their folks, began to imitate my parents. The boy dragged one leg in an exaggerated limp, like a monster in a cheap horror film. The girl formed her arms into a huge circle, puffed out her cheeks, and waddled with great effort. The father pretended to shush the children, but he silently laughed his encouragement. The mother cupped her hand over her mouth to hide her expression of half giggle, half disgust.

In the past I'd seen people stare or maybe look at us for longer than a polite glance, but this was different. My family didn't seem to notice or be bothered by it.

But I did. Something happened in me. I felt a sharp pain in my heart and, as best a five-year-old could understand them, mingled feelings of righteous anger, injustice, and flat-out hurt feelings. Something like a sob erupted deep inside me. I kept the lid on it; I didn't make a sound. But I can still remember feeling my chest cave, my breath catch, my eyes burn, and my throat tighten.

*What are these people doing?* I asked myself. *Why are they looking at us? Why would they be imitating Mom and Dad? Why would they do that?* Perplexed and unnerved, I looked over at my family. And there for the first time I saw them—really *saw* them—as everyone else saw them.

Daddy's twisted and ungainly gait, his foot wrenched at a forty-five degree angle, his shriveled leg, which looked more like a young girl's wrist than a grown man's limb—ever-present reminders of a toddler's battle with polio.

Mom's obesity. Countless years of countless diets and five-hundred-calories-a-day monitored hospital stays, only to gain yet more weight, develop yet more arthritis in her knees, and suffer yet more debilitating pain.

*Fat is the last preserve for unexamined bigotry.* —*Jennifer Coleman*

My brother's towering height and battle with his weight. Through the years diabetes has taken its toll, as amputations have whittled away his mobility and left him with an artificial foot.

I felt conspicuous too, with my knobby knees, thick glasses, and ghostly white-and-freckled skin. But even at age five I realized that the way people reacted to me paled in comparison to the judgments they leveled at my mom, dad, and brother. So I watched this family I didn't know make fun of the family I knew and loved so well. And it hurt.

Yes, my family was different. But they are the most beautiful people I've ever seen. From them I learned what true beauty is.

My Daddy is gone now, but he was the strongest, kindest man I'd ever known. He set the standard for what I looked for—and found—in a husband. Dad never viewed himself as "handicapped"—he hated the word. His massive torso was evidence of his strength, the strength that built—from the ground up—the house I grew up in. Though he was often in great pain, I never heard a word of complaint. He lived with grace and died with dignity. He was honest and good and true.

Mom is in a wheelchair now, but she has more spirit and optimism and humor than anyone I know. Accomplished and creative, she casts a wide net of love and encouragement to everyone around her.

At six feet four inches tall, my brother, Tracy, has always stood head and shoulders above the crowd. Nobody who knew him was surprised when he became a city concilman, then mayor, and then spent ten years in Florida's House of Representatives. This gentle giant has a natural brilliance, a quiet courage, and a gentle kindness that belies his stature.

Through the years, if Mom and Dad and Tracy have noticed the pointing and the laughter and the snickers, you would never know it. No knee-jerk reactions. No angry retorts. Just quiet nobility. They have always responded in good nature to offense, extending grace to the ignorant, showing dignity in the face of cruelty, and meeting heartache with humor. Their spirit and intelligence and tenderness and humor have risen above the limits of their physical bodies. They have laughed and loved and given and sacrificed. My family is what beauty looks like.

Man looks at the outward appearance, but the Lord looks at the heart.

It thrills me to imagine what God thinks when He looks upon the hearts of my family. I can just hear Him exclaim: "You are so beautiful to Me!"

*The criterion of true beauty is that it increases on examination;*
*if false, that it lessens.——Lord Grenville*

## REFLECTIONS OF HIS LOVE

I just read these words by C. S. Lewis...and I never want to forget them!

It is a serious thing to live in a society of possible gods and goddesses, to remember that the dullest and most uninteresting person you talk to may one day be a creature which, if you saw it now, you would be strongly tempted to worship, or else a horror and a corruption such as you now meet, if at all, only in a nightmare. It is in the light of these overwhelming possibilities...with awe and circumspection...that we should conduct all our dealings with one another.... There are no *ordinary* people. You have never talked to a mere mortal.[3]

O Lord,

thank You that You do not judge as we judge.

You do not judge us by mere appearances.

Keep me from judging that way too, Lord.

Even when I know You, when I know the truth,

I often don't see things right.

Forgive me, Father. Give me Your eyes to see as You see.

Open the eyes of my understanding;

increase my discernment.

Show me the true beauty of those around me

when I am apt to miss it.

Let who I am on the inside always be more important to me

than how I look on the outside.

May my appearance never deceive.

Keep my heart pure before You.

When You look upon me, may my heart be pleasing to You.

Amen

# CHAPTER TWO

# THE ULTIMATE MAKEOVER

# The Beauty of Brokenness

He is near me...

*The Lord is close to the brokenhearted,
and saves those who are crushed in spirit.* ——*Psalm 34:18*

You still might be thinking...

*A beauty book? I have more substantial things to read. This isn't spiritual enough. This isn't important enough. I'm not interested.*

Let's be honest. Even if you lead two Bible studies and can recite half the New Testament, you might be feeling self-conscious about your battle with your weight or those little lines beginning to creep around your eyes.

You could be a doctor or the CEO of a Fortune 500 company but still struggle with feelings of insecurity and inadequacy.

Perhaps you're a young woman who should be embracing all the exciting possibilities that lie before you as you discover your uniqueness, but instead you're being held hostage to a media standard that drives you to secret obsessions that make you feel guilty and ashamed.

Maybe you just don't feel very beautiful. Maybe your shape is more round than lean, or maybe you're saying, "Look, I'm not twenty years old any more, and I'm more a size 2X than a 2. Why should I be interested in beauty?"

Or you could have a face like Michelle Pfeiffer, a figure that Julia Roberts would envy, and be the most popular "belle of the ball"…but still feel "less than." Though the rest of the world may think you have it all, you know better. Because of the pain of your early life, ridicule, or feelings of rejection, when you look in the mirror, all you see is what's wrong with you.

Do you feel beautiful? If not, why not?

Do you feel worthless, unaccepted, unloved, misunderstood?

Are there things in your life or from your past that cause you shame and pain?

Maybe through abuse someone you once trusted took away your innocence…and with it a part of yourself. Or maybe it was the abandonment you experienced when a parent left, either through divorce or neglect or death. Maybe it's hard for you to imagine that your worth is based on who you *are* rather than on what you *do*.

Have painful experiences like these made it hard for you to believe and receive the deep truth that God loves you, accepts you, delights in you, and cherishes you?

Even as I sat down to write this book, full of enthusiasm and certain that its message would bring freedom to women, I was hit with the same ol' stuff:

*I'm a fraud. Who am I to speak to women about this? I feel about as ugly right now as I have at any time in my life—emotionally, spiritually, and physically. How dare I try to write about this subject? I look around me. Every single person seems better—more creative, more anointed, more successful, more everything. Unlike me, they're moving forward in the things of God. I spiral downward. What have I really accomplished lately? I lack discipline, I'm blue, I'm weak, I feel stripped bare, and frankly, my response is not "Praise God!" My circumstances are lousy, and I don't like myself right now.*

Whheeeww, I feel better.

They say to write what we know. I thought I knew. But I find I'm still learning.

One of the reasons I want to share my story with you is that, though I may have *done* very different things than you, I think that inside we might be a lot alike. I've had a recurring theme in my life. It's called rejection. I know that many of you have probably had far more severe and damaging wounds than I have ever experienced or could even imagine. But I also know that any wound, any hurt that keeps us from being all the Lord created us to be, is an area He wants to touch and heal.

I've already told you about my experience in ballet class when I was in the first grade. Scene change: Cut to high school. Not much improvement. Still unattractive, gawky, gangly, but at least my Coke-bottle-thick glasses were brown instead of blue.

I was shy, unpopular, and very straight—didn't go to parties, didn't drink. My nickname through high school was "Super Virgin." The girls laughed at me; the boys whispered about me. My "social circle" consisted of other rejects. The only boys who asked me for dates were guys that even I, a fellow geek, couldn't bring myself to go out with.

My mother is very gracious and altruistic, and she lives the principle of preferring others to self. So once, in an effort to improve my social life as well as teach me the value of giving sacrificially to others, she said, "Nancy, you're such a fine person. Nobody else will go to the Key Club dance with Don. If you won't go with him, he won't get to go at all. Can't you just do it for him?"

Now, I love my mother dearly, but she was asking a lot of me! Mom didn't realize that Don was *the* geek in class, an even bigger one than I was, and that instead of helping my reputation, going to the dance with him would totally annihilate whatever shred of self-esteem I had left. But I wanted to please...and I also sincerely wanted to do the kind and generous thing. So I went to the dance with Don.

A few weeks later all the social clubs at school inducted their new members. My two equally dorky girlfriends and I —we were dubbed the "tragic trio"—had applied for the very worst club in the school, the lowest rung on the social ladder. Only a handful of people belonged to it, so we figured we'd at least have a shot at that one!

On "rush" day I got all dressed up, sat down in a chair by the dining room window, and waited, listening for the honking horns as the cars came by to pick up their lucky new members. Finally, *finally,* I heard the horns signaling their arrival. I was so excited! They picked up my friend next door. They picked up my friend across the street. Then they drove away. I sat at the window for almost another hour, thinking: *They've just forgotten; surely they'll be coming back.*

The next day at my locker I was cut to the quick when I over-heard one of my friends from the tragic trio say to her new club mate, "There's no way Nancy could ever be in our club. She goes out with dorks…and she's so ugly."

Rejection. And it doesn't happen just in childhood, does it? I'm still amazed that I chose a profession where I experience rejection almost on a daily basis! It happens even today. Recently I auditioned for a delightful part in a TV movie—a mom in her forties with a young teenager. It was a wonderful script and I had a great reading, which, frankly, I don't usually say. But I knew I was right for the role, and I nailed the audition. Afterward I called my agent to tell her how excited I was and to ask her to get feedback from the director.

When she called me back, she kind of hemmed and hawed, and then she stammered, "Um…Nancy…yes, he said you did a great read-ing, the best they saw…but, um…um…how…how…old are you?"

"I'm forty-four," I said, "and you submit me for roles from midthirties to midforties."

"Yeah, yeah, I know," she said. "That's what I thought. I told the director you were in your early forties, but he said, 'You've got to be kidding! She looks at *least* fifty-five!'"

*Well...fifty-five isn't so bad,* I thought. *Just not yet!* And all the memories of rejection from first grade through high school came flooding back: *"You're ugly. You're clumsy. We don't want you."*

We've all had experiences of pain and rejection. The world has at times pushed us away, judging us or those we love based on our appearance or popularity or social acceptance. But God sees our hearts. He knows our need...and draws us near.

# Beauty for Ashes

He heals me...

*I have heard your prayer and seen your tears;*
*I will heal you.*—2 *Kings* 20:5

FEELINGS OF REJECTION followed me through high school, and by the time I graduated, I had pretty much given up trying to reconcile the kind of girl I thought God wanted me to be with what I saw around me. In my frustration and confusion I quit going to church, and I remained a prodigal for almost fifteen years.

In college, I began to blossom...finally. I grew into my five-foot-nine-inch frame. The years of braces began to pay off, the glasses gave way to contacts, and a long-awaited figure finally emerged. Boys began to notice, and their attention made me feel good about myself for the first time. I went full-bore into the dating scene, lapping up male approval like a hungry puppy. My insecurities and low self-image were still there; they were just hidden behind the facade of "pretty" and "popular."

I didn't become wild or promiscuous, but I did begin to try to meet the need I had for approval and acceptance with boyfriends. I went from one relationship to the next, lining up the new boyfriend before ending the current romance. I gave myself no time to reflect on who I was or what I really wanted—I was too insecure and afraid to be alone.

Through the years it wasn't always men that filled the void. Sometimes it was things—possessions, houses, cars, achievements, success, money, fame—or whatever I thought would fill the empty places inside me where I still felt inadequate and unworthy.

After college I became Miss Florida and competed in the Miss America Pageant. A modeling and commercial career in New York followed. I landed my first TV series on my first audition, the first of five series I've starred in over the past twenty years. As I sailed through my career, success just seemed to follow in my wake. I certainly didn't get everything I auditioned for, but I got a lot. It was heady. It was happening fast and furious. And I became much more self-sufficient, self-reliant, and even self-confident.

But at the age of twenty-five, when I was at the height of my modeling career and beginning another one in acting, my secure new world threatened to come crashing down: I was diagnosed with a severe skin cancer on my face. In the hospital a surgeon took my hands in his and said, "Now, I can't guarantee what you're going to look like after surgery, so if I were you, I'd have an alternate career in mind."

It hit me like a shot. Yes, I was terrified of the surgery, but I was even more horrified by how important my face and body had become to me. My mother's words haunted me: *Nancy, honey, you're so beautiful on the inside. That's what counts.* With my history, how could my priorities have gotten so skewed?

The very source of ridicule and rejection in my life—my physical self—had become the basis of my affirmation. Having grown up feeling insecure, self-conscious, and rejected, I now made my profession in the most insecure, rejection-prone industry on the planet. The irony didn't escape me. Maybe my bottom-line problem was masochism! Or…maybe I had just been searching for the kind of absolute acceptance that only God could give, trying in vain to fill the emptiness that only He could fill.

I was humbled and ashamed, and that day I began to hunger for God again.

But I didn't want Christianity. I figured that there surely had to be more, and for several years I looked for it in Eastern religions and New Age philosophies. It was an eclectic search. I read the Bible every day, along with the Bhagavad Gita, the Koran, and the *Course in Miracles,* diligently searching for the truth.

Meanwhile, my career continued to flourish. For three years I had a starring role in the series *St. Elsewhere* and guest-starring roles on numerous shows. Then one day when I was on my way to the airport to shoot an episode of *Magnum P.I.* in Honolulu, I stopped by my mailbox. A book I'd ordered had arrived, so I popped it in my satchel and headed off to Hawaii. When I arrived, I discovered that someone in production scheduling had made a mistake: They'd brought me in three days early. So I had nothing to do for three full days but read the book I'd brought, *Power for Living,* a collection of Christian testimonies with a foreword by Jamie Buckingham.

God had made an appointment with me.

As I read the stories, one after another, of people's encounters with God, a pain I didn't even realize I had began welling up inside my heart. It was an actual physical pain, and it was so deep that I honestly thought I was going to die. In every story people described the very thing I so desperately needed and wanted. They had a relationship with God, and even though I had been searching for Him, I had come up empty. And it broke my heart.

I fell on my face sobbing before God. I saw myself clearly for the first time in years. I saw my emptiness and knew that my life was a sham. Even though it may have looked as if I had it all, my deep loneliness, feelings of inferiority, and fear kept feeding my need for more—more success, more acceptance, more money, more…everything. I saw the brokenness of my life. I saw the consequences of all my bad choices and how I had tried to fill the void inside me with men and things and status. I saw my sin, and I was destitute. I needed Him!

Finally, all alone on a beach in Hawaii, I encountered the One who had been there all along. I cried out to Him from the depths of my pain, and He answered, ministering to me in such a way that, to this day, I've never experienced anything as powerful.

He showed me things about Himself and about myself.

He showed me what He thought of me, how much He loved me, how much He'd missed me. He reminded me about that little girl long ago who had known Him so well. I actually felt His broken heart for me.

Then He showed me who He is, what His real nature is—that He is not only the Creator of the universe, but also my loving Father. He showed me how far He had gone to bring me back to Himself, how He had consistently and unconditionally pursued me, even when I was running away from Him. He showed me that what He wanted more than anything else was a relationship with me.

And then, the most powerful of all, He showed me the truth of who His Son is—that Jesus isn't just a great prophet or a role model or a good man. He is the living God, and He had bought me with a price. He had given Himself for me—unworthy, unlovely me. Amazing!

For three days I lay on my face on the floor of my hotel room sobbing, first in grief and repentance, and then in absolute joy and gratitude, as the Lord flooded me with incredible peace. It was as if I had grabbed onto His sleeve and wouldn't let Him go. I was a prodigal child rushing back into her Father's arms. I was home! The most loving, tender, gentle, gracious presence I had ever encountered came over me, and I felt sweetly whole, utterly safe and secure, and completely accepted. That day, God began to heal the broken places inside me, restore my distorted self-perception, and fill my hungry heart.

Sometimes our greatest need is not at the level of awareness. It looked as if I had everything—a flourishing career, wealth, romance. But at my core my need was for God, not goods; for inner cleanness, loveliness, and wholeness, not outward beauty.

After that life-changing encounter I went back to L.A. and prayed for acting work I could be proud of…and for a husband who would love God above all else. A Disney family series, *Sidekicks,* soon followed, as did the *Matlock* series, a string of TV movies, and *Main Floor,* the fashion/beauty magazine show I've hosted for more than eight years. And finally, though I had almost given up hope that my prayer for a husband would ever be answered, when I was thirty-five, I married Larry Myers, the amazing man God had in mind for me.

God has given me the ultimate makeover, and every day He gives me beauty for ashes as He continues to heal, restore, and transform me.

*God, give me a broken heart, if that is where*
*Your healing can start.*—James Langteaux

# REFLECTIONS OF HIS LOVE

Incredible day of prayer, tears, feeling Him all over me, actually overcoming me, my own current weakness, lack of faith, failure in my responses to Larry and my circumstances. Yet He's coming closer to me, not repelled by me. The more I cry out to Him to help me, the weaker and more frail and useless and hopeless I feel, the more I cry out in need, the closer He comes.

It's the opposite of what we expect from the world. The needier I am, the more He rushes in. He's breaking down my performance-oriented personality. And my perfectionism. With Him, it's not how well I do, how good I look on the surface, how well I pretend to know what I'm doing, or how much I look like I have it all together.

When I break, when I'm shattered, when I fail, when I can't get anything right, *when I can't stand myself*—that's when He floods me with His mercy and grace, and I feel Him standing over me, admiring me, saying, *"Now* you look beautiful to Me! Now I can come to you and give you all that you desire. Now My life can flow in you—because there are empty places that I will fill with My life, My love, My strength, My righteousness, My holiness. Now there's room for Me in you. It was too crowded before."

Lord,

I am naked before You,

stripped of everything I do to make You love me.

When I'm still not the person I want to be,

when I fail again and again and again,

thank You that You never leave me, even then.

You know that my deepest need is for You,

and when I run from You,

You still pursue me and draw me near.

When everyone else leaves, You come!

It's almost too much for me to fathom.

Thank You for the gift of brokenness,

the privilege of emptiness.

I am beginning to understand Your life in me,

Your beauty for my ashes.

Come by Your Spirit now,

and heal the broken places within me.

Amen

# CHAPTER THREE

# A HEALING BALM

# A Clear Picture

### He bears my pain…

*Surely he has borne our griefs and carried our sorrows. . . . He was wounded for our transgressions, he was bruised for our iniquities; upon him was the chastisement that made us whole.*—*Isaiah* 53:4–5, *RSV*

A FEW YEARS AGO, I attended a conference on Christian healing. After a terrific teaching on the power of Christ to enter our injured places and heal the wounds of the past, the speaker asked the group to be quiet before the Lord for a few minutes and invite Him to show us something that needed healing, an emotional residue from the past that needed His touch.

The entire room grew silent in private prayer. I was quiet for a moment, but nothing came to me. I waited another minute or so. Nothing. Getting a bit restless, I stole a peek around the room. It seemed as though almost everyone was experiencing a beautiful moment with the Lord. Tears flowing, peaceful expressions. Me, nothing.

Then all of a sudden a picture flitted past. I was in third grade. Crooked pigtails, protruding teeth, and big, thick glasses. In this fleeting picture I was in the classroom with all the kids and my teacher, Mrs. Hadnott. (She was appropriately named—I always wished I *had not* had her!)

I'd been legally blind since who knows when, and I'd just gotten this new pair of glasses that were as thick as the bottom of Coke bottles and magnified my already big, round eyes. I looked like Don Knotts in the movie *The Incredible Mr. Limpett*. But the doctor had given me the wrong prescription; so even with my new thick glasses, I couldn't see past my elbow. Every time I needed to read the blackboard, I had to get out of my seat and go to the front of the classroom. Since we were seated alphabetically, I was in the back of the room, and I made lots of visits to the blackboard. With each trip, the kids whooped and teased, "Sit down. C'mon, outta the way. Not again! Move your big fat head!" Even Mrs. Hadnott seemed more exasperated than usual.

So that was the memory that flitted past: classmates taunting a shy, insecure eight-year-old in Coke-bottle glasses. Yes, it was humiliating and embarrassing, but it certainly wasn't the worst thing that had ever happened to me. It seemed *insignificant*. So I ignored it.

But just then, the speaker went to the microphone and said, "Even if it seems *insignificant*, if the Lord brings it to your mind, pray about it." So I did. *Lord, what are You saying? What are You trying to show me?* And another picture came to my mind.

Jesus came into my classroom. He walked across the front of the room, came straight down my row, and stopped right beside my chair. He reached out, took my hand in His, and walked with me to the front of the room to read the blackboard. Behind us, the classroom got very quiet; the laughing and jeering had stopped. And when I turned around, Mrs. Hadnott and all the kids were smiling at me with approval and acceptance. I couldn't believe it! I looked up at Jesus. He was smiling too. And He was wearing big, thick, Coke-bottle glasses that magnified His eyes—just like mine did! Standing in front of the class, we both laughed.

I smiled through tears when I saw that picture. Only God could show me something that personal, that funny…and that profound.

In that moment, He showed me that I was created in His image and that He would go to any length to remind me of my identity. He showed me what He thought of me and how much He loved and accepted me. But even more, that image of *Him* wearing *my* glasses pierced my heart with a staggering revelation: Jesus was not only willing to die for me; He was willing to bear my humiliation and embarrassment. *He was willing to wear my glasses!*

Jesus wants to carry our pain Himself. We forget that He not only "healed" us by taking up our sins, but that He also took up and wants to bear all of our "infirmities." He cared about my pain from the long-forgotten past and wanted to touch me with healing there. But He also literally wanted *to take my place,* to carry it Himself, to bear my chastisement.

That day I felt as though I had a deeper understanding of what the writer of Hebrews meant when he said that Jesus was made like you and me "in every way":

> That's why he had to enter into every detail of human life. Then, when he came before God as high priest to get rid of the people's sins, he would have already experienced it all himself—all the pain, all the testing—and would be able to help where help was needed.
>
> HEBREWS 2:17–18, *THE MESSAGE*

Your hurt might have nothing to do with classroom taunts or Coke-bottle glasses. It might be something less, or something much, much deeper and much more traumatic and heartbreaking. But whatever it is that has hurt you, damaged you, or caused you shame—*even if it seems insignificant*—Jesus wants not only to heal you there, but also to bear the pain for you.

The pain of your past is accessible to the Spirit of God, who is not bound by time and space. Jesus understands. He identifies with our pain. He bears our grief and carries our sorrows. He heals. He will show you, just as He showed me, that He will go to any length to remind you of His great love for you.

Sit quietly before Jesus and allow Him to show you that He knows everything about you: every time you were hurting, every time you were lonely, every time you were afraid. Let Him fill in all that was spiritually and emotionally missing at that time. Let Him come to those places in your life where, even now, you need His healing touch. Let Him take your place, let Him bear your pain, let Him carry your shame…let Him wear your glasses.

Although I didn't know it, the ridicule of my teacher and classmates had left an emotional residue. But Jesus knew, and He showed me one more thing that day: I had to forgive them. The negative effects of that situation—and my lack of forgiveness—needed to come to the Cross.

*Without memory there is no healing.*
*Without forgiveness there is no future.*—*Desmond Tutu*

## REFLECTIONS OF HIS LOVE

In confessing my black heart, my terrible reactions to things, I began weeping.

God said, "I love you and am so proud of you."

*How can You be, Lord, with these things in my heart?*

"Because you are at your weakest right now. You are so self-sufficient, even hard. But now...do you need Me?"

*Yes, Lord,* through tears.

"These are just your feelings. Don't be ashamed of them. I'm not. I created you to feel. Allow yourself to feel them—*then* bring them under My reign and rule. Feel them first, then submit them to Me."

# THE POWER TO FORGIVE

He gives me power...

*I pray also that the eyes of your heart may be enlightened in order that you may know...his incomparably great power for us who believe.——Ephesians 1:18—19*

IF SOMETHING AS long-ago and forgotten as an offense in third grade had resided in my soul and occupied even a smidgen of my heart for so long, how much more unforgivingness did I harbor? *I want my heart to be clean before You, Lord.* I prayed. *I want nothing between You and me.*

I sat quietly before God and asked Him to open the eyes of my heart and show me my unforgivingness. Soon He brought to my mind a name here, a face there, a recollection of a long-held grievance here, a memory of an offense there. It was slow at first. Then they came tumbling out—people, places, times, and events—some long ago, some as recent as that morning. He reminded me of people who had wronged me intentionally as well as those who had hurt me without meaning to and who would be heartsick to know they had.

I thought of Paul's word to the Romans: "If it is possible, as far as it depends on you, live at peace with everyone" (Romans 12:18). We're to live in harmony with one another, Paul says, and bless those who persecute us.

So one by one as God brought them to mind, I forgave, as best

I could, mistreatments and insults and snubs. And with each confession and repentance and release, *I* felt released. I felt freed from
the exhaustion of bearing so many offenses, and I was surprised and
ashamed at how long I'd carried some of them. That day marked
another giant step in the deep healing of my soul.

I admit that there are a couple of wrongs I'm still having trouble
with. I think I've forgiven and blessed them, only to have my emotions rise up again in indignation and outrage. When that happens,
I drag myself back to the altar and climb up. And when my pride
makes me think that I'm justified in my anger or unforgivingness, I
only have to remember how much God has forgiven me. Then I
think of Jesus' conversation with Peter: "'Lord, how many times shall
I forgive my brother when he sins against me? Up to seven times?'
Jesus answered, 'I tell you, not seven times, but seventy-seven times'"
(Matthew 18:21–22).

Gulp.

I find I have to read Paul a lot these days: "Bear with each other
and forgive whatever grievances you may have against one another.
Forgive as the Lord forgave you" (Colossians 3:13).

We forgive because God commands us to, not because we feel
like it. When we choose to forgive, God does a work of grace in us.
But it's our forgiveness that sets the process in motion. It may come
in stages, but no real healing can occur without it. The Holy Spirit
tenderly prompts us to repent of our own sin if we need to and helps
us to forgive others—whether we feel like it or not.

No matter what people do to us, we are responsible to forgive
them from our hearts, as God has forgiven us, and to repent of any
of our own sinful reactions to whatever was done to us. We will never
heal and really become whole until we stop blaming others or our
circumstances for our pain.

*He who cannot forgive another breaks the bridge over which he must pass himself.*—George Herbert

The hurt I feel may still be present, but as I forgive, I begin to view the incident from God's perspective, and a unique thing takes place: I gain insight into it. It's no longer just about *me;* I begin to see the pain and brokenness in the lives of those who have wounded me. And I find that the more I see the things that I do and recognize my own sin and weakness, the more I begin to understand why others act the way they do.

A pastor once shared with me some important steps to begin the process of healing. I'd like to pass them on to you.

First, ask God to show you who or what is at the root of your hurt, and then tell Him exactly how you feel about whoever sinned against you. Don't be afraid, and don't hold anything back. Be completely honest. God knows how you feel in the deepest part of your heart anyway; you're not keeping anything from Him. All you're doing is finally being completely open and frank about your feelings.

That's what King David did. He often poured out his feelings in psalms, showing us by example that we can tell God anything, even if it doesn't seem very "spiritual" to us:

In his arrogance the wicked man hunts down the
weak…in all his thoughts there is no room for God. His
ways are always prosperous; he is haughty and your laws
are far from him; he sneers at all his enemies. Break the
arm of the wicked and evil man; call him to account for
his wickedness that would not be found out.

PSALM 10:2, 4–5, 15

How long, O LORD? Will you forget me forever? How
long will you hide your face from me?… How long will
my enemy triumph over me?

PSALM 13:1–2

Don't worry. You can be honest with God. He can take it. You're
not going to drive Him away.

After you've poured out your heart to God, make a conscious
decision to forgive every word, action, or attitude of whoever hurt
you. Remember that this is not about feelings; it's about obedience
and trusting that God *in* us has the power *for* us to forgive, based on
the blood of Christ.

As you begin to pray and forgive, more offenses that need to be
forgiven might come to mind, as they did with me. When you forgive and release those who have hurt you, you're not only releasing
them, you're also releasing yourself from bitterness and resentment.
You're freeing yourself from their control and breaking loose from
the bondage of unforgivingness.

Now, if there is any judgment you've made against those people,
renounce it and ask God *not only* to forgive them for their sin against
you, *but also* to bless them and fill them with His love. Then ask God
to forgive you for your own sinful reactions toward them—your lack
of forgiveness, bitterness, anger, gossip, judgment, resentment, or
wishing them ill. This is an important part of the process because, in
the long run, we are often hurt far more by our unresolved, sinful
reactions than by the initial hurt itself. And (you're being honest,
remember?) ask God to forgive you for judging Him or being bitter
or angry toward Him for having allowed that pain in your life in the
first place.

Ask the Holy Spirit to come into those areas in your heart and
memory and heal them. His very presence heals. He can redeem the

sorrow and turn to good what Satan meant for evil. Let what happened, now redeemed and renewed, drive you into an even deeper and more intimate relationship with the Divine Healer. As the presence of Christ replaces the pain of the past, as you see what He does in your life and emotions, gratitude will overwhelm you, and all that you've been through will enable you to comfort others with the comfort you have received.

Practice forgiveness as part of your daily lifestyle, keeping a short account with the Lord as He brings people and situations to mind from which He wants to free you. God can remind you of the unresolved issues hidden in your heart. As He did with me, He can bring to mind people who have wounded you, either long ago or just yesterday.

Only we can forgive those who have hurt us. But when we do, forgiveness breaks the power of sin and opens the door to our prison. It shatters the walls of anger, guilt, and shame that keep us from God and from others.

God has abundantly blessed my career. He has given me favor in the entertainment industry and wonderful success. But all of that pales in comparison to what He's been doing inside of me: healing my heart, mind, and spirit of past rejections, low self-image, insecurities, and inadequacies. Freeing me. And that's what He wants to do with you.

*Only a small crack but cracks*
*make caves collapse.——Alexander Solzhenitsyn*

Lord,

I thank You that I can come to You

with my feelings, my anger, my resentments.

Show me my unforgivingness.

Show me those I am still holding hostage.

Father, help me choose to forgive them.

And forgive me, Lord, for my own sinful judgments. . .

even my judgment of You.

Thank You for the forgiveness You have given me.

I want a clean heart before You, Lord.

Help me to forgive as I have been forgiven.

Help me to be free.

Amen

# CHAPTER FOUR

# A DIVINE
## MASTERPIECE

# GOD'S WORKMANSHIP

I am His workmanship…

*O Lord, you are our Father. We are the clay, you are the potter;*
*we are all the work of your hand.—Isaiah 64:8*

A HUGE BLOCK OF marble eighteen feet high was given to a sculptor. But the marble was flawed, and as Agostino di Duccio began to carve, he realized that he could do nothing with the block of stone. So it sat gathering dust for forty years. Then twenty-six-year-old Michelangelo saw something in the marble.

A little boy watched Michelangelo carefully sculpt the stone. After many days, many weeks, many months, the famous form of David began to appear. Finally, the little boy tugged on Michelangelo's cloak and asked, "Sir, how did you know he was in there?"

Michelangelo replied, "I just took away everything that wasn't David."

So it is with us. God is creating us; we are His work of art. Before He formed you in your mother's womb, He knew you. Before He laid the foundations of the earth, before the beginning of time, He already had you in mind. He created you as a unique treasure, a beautiful work of art. He knows who you are. He sees your worth and uniqueness and beauty. And like Michelangelo, all He has to do is take away the parts that don't belong to reveal the masterpiece that is you.

The first step toward becoming who we are meant to be is to receive Jesus' gift of mercy and forgiveness of sin. When we pray a simple prayer, admitting that we're sinners who have fallen short, asking forgiveness, and acknowledging that Jesus paid the price for our sin with His death and resurrection, we enter into new life. Maybe you've never really done that before. Or maybe you know Christ as your Savior, but you've never allowed Him to be Lord of your life. Or perhaps you're like I was for so many years—living apart from God. But you know in your heart that He is drawing you back, just waiting for you to give your whole life to Him.

No matter how worthless or unlovely we may feel, He comes close, drawing us to Himself without reservation or judgment. The Bible tells us that "there is now no condemnation for those who are in Christ Jesus" (Romans 8:1). There is no accusation, no blame— only unconditional love as He transforms you into His own image.

Master Sculptor that He is, little by little, carefully and tenderly, God begins to chisel away everything that hides the work of art beneath. Because He loves you so dearly, He pares away everything that is hiding your true self, until, more and more, it emerges—the beautiful masterpiece He created you to be. That's what Jesus did with Simon Peter. He called His disciple "the rock" long before Peter became it. He saw something within Peter: He saw what he would become. And Jesus called him out.

Jesus is calling you out too. He sees something in the rock that encases you. He sees who you are and who you will become in Him. Like anything of great beauty and worth, it doesn't happen overnight. But it does happen over a lifetime, as you allow Him to sculpt you into the beautiful, unique woman He designed you to be.

The figure of David came alive only after thousands and thousands—tens of thousands—of perfectly directed hard and soft blows. But it yielded a work of unparalleled beauty. If Michelangelo could chisel away stone and reveal a David, just think what the Creator of the universe can pare away and reveal in you!

Marble carving is difficult and precise and takes time. It's hard work. But it is the sculptor's work—the stone just rests in the artist's hands. Will you rest in God's hands and let Him heal your insecurities and feelings of unworthiness? Will you let Him fill all the needs you've tried to fill with possessions or relationships, busyness or success, with food or alcohol or drugs? Will you let Him show you that you no longer have to be a people pleaser who always needs to give the "right impression" or a perfectionist who needs to get everything "just right"? Will you let Him show you that He accepts you completely and loves you unconditionally?

God is the potter...we are the clay. God is the sculptor...we are the smooth stone. As we allow Him to, He gently chisels away what covers us, and with every layer He removes, we see the real us emerging: new aspects of our personality, new talents, radiant confidence, unshakable security.

This is your opportunity. This is your time for wholeness and healing. Jesus is calling you out.

*He's been a waiten there in the wood*
*you might say since before I was born.*
*I jist brung him out a little——but one a these days,*
*jist you wait an see, we'll find the time an a face fer him an bring*
*him out a that block.——Harriette Arnow*

# GOD'S WORK

He sets me free...

*If the Son sets you free,*
*you will be free indeed.——John 8:36*

THE FAILURES OF OTHERS—parents, spouses, children, friends, bosses—affect all of us. If we're honest, we have to say that at times even God disappoints us terribly. And, wounded, we often react by believing lies: *God doesn't really love me. If He loved me, why would He allow this to happen to me? I must deserve it. I'm worthless. I'm disgusting. I'm stupid....*

What we think and believe determines how we act or react. If we believe a lie, it perverts the way we see *everything,* and out of fear we develop all kinds of defense mechanisms—things like control, passivity, or compulsive behaviors—to hide, to protect ourselves, or just to survive.

Satan loves to use our pasts against us. Have you ever noticed how many of the words used to describe his character start with the prefix *de* or *dis?* The Bible says that he *de*stroys, *de*ceives, *dis*courages. I looked up the definition of these prefixes. *De* means "to reduce," as in *de*grade; *dis* means "to deprive of, remove, exclude," as in *dis*-courage. Satan *de*ceives, *dis*appoints, *dis*illusions, *de*feats. His sole purpose is to isolate and destroy us, either emotionally or physically.

Jesus, on the other hand, loves to make our pasts work for us. His character is revealed in the prefix *re,* meaning "to go back again or to return to the starting place." Jesus *re*deems, *re*conciles, *re*freshes, *re*stores, *re*news, *re*vives, *re*surrects. Through His Son, our heavenly Father gets us back to the place where things went wrong and gives us a new beginning. The Holy Spirit wants to apply the *re*storative power of Jesus to the *de*struction of the enemy.

At the cross, God laid on Jesus the compressed weight of all my sin: my guilt and shame and all my sorrows and pain. He became sin for me—my own sins and the sins committed against me—and died my death. The worship song "At the Cross" describes perfectly what Christ has done.

## AT THE CROSS

I know a place
A wonderful place
Where accused and condemned
Find mercy and grace
Where the wrongs we have done
and the wrongs done to us
Were nailed there with You
There at the cross.

At the cross
You died for our sins
At the cross
You gave us life again.

Words and music by Randy Butler and Terry Butler (ASCAP).
© 1993 Mercy/Vineyard Publishing. Used by permission.

Once we put our trust in Christ's work at the cross, He frees us from the lies that once gave us our identity. He takes all that away. "I have been crucified with Christ," wrote the apostle Paul, "and I no longer live, but Christ lives in me" (Galatians 2:20). I am a new creation in Christ, and I have a new identity. I'm not who I was—I am Christ in me!

Are you still believing the lies? If so, it doesn't matter what you *do*—you might be an actress, a doctor, or even a minister—those lies still dictate who you think you *are*. Well, God wants to break the power of those lies and set you free to believe and live in His truth.

Paul tells us: "We are God's workmanship, created in Christ Jesus to do good works, which God prepared in advance for us to do" (Ephesians 2:10). God calls you a new creation, His divine masterpiece, a work of art. That's what God thinks of you; that's who you *really* are.

# TEARING DOWN THE WALL

He rescues me...

*"Because he loves me," says the Lord,*
*"I will rescue him."* ——*Psalm 91:14*

THE NEGATIVE THINGS said to and about us stick. Like a broken record, they play over and over in the wounded part of us, making it impossible for us to hear whatever positive things people might say.

And with every rejection and hurt, we put up another wall to fortify ourselves against the pain. *Here in this safe place I can't be rejected,* we tell ourselves. *Here I have control.* But those walls don't really keep others out, because their hurtful words still affect us, don't they? Instead, the walls keep us locked in, imprisoned by lies and fear.

God delights in the heart that wants to move closer and closer to Him. He eagerly rushes toward the one who wants a deeper understanding and intimacy with Him. But sometimes we can have barriers that prevent us from seeing God as He is and ourselves as He sees us.

I've told you about being an unattractive, bucktoothed little girl with Coke-bottle glasses. Remember the story I told you about when

I was six years old? When I heard the teacher of my ballet class say that I was "the clumsiest, most awkward child" she'd ever seen? Well, that was when I put up my first wall of protection. As the years passed and I faced more rejection, I put up plenty of others.

We can have walls that we don't even realize we've built. The Lord wants to free that woman in all of us that still feels like a little child who has been rejected and hurt. He wants to remove anything that obscures our real selves. He wants to take us out of our hiding places and into His light. God wants to *tear down* the walls.

It's only as we allow the truth of His light to shine into the hurting and closed-off places that we become whole and free. And then, secure in His love and acceptance, we become mature women, able to walk in the fullness of who He created us to be.

*The shell must be cracked apart if what is in it is to come out, for if you want the kernel, you must break the shell.*—*Meister Eckhart*

When I was preparing for a women's retreat recently, I prayed, as I always do, *Lord, what do these women need from You?* I sensed that they were a group committed to His church but unacquainted with His intimacy. I felt as though God said, *They need what you need. Tell them what I've told you so many times: "Just rest in Me. Let Me show My love to you."* And then I had this picture in my mind....

I saw a woman standing behind a short brick wall. She was very strong, very confident and self-assured, very in control of herself, even rather imposing in body and voice. Her mind was sharp, and she seemed to be fearless, but she was building a brick wall to protect herself. The bricks had words written on them: cynicism, sarcasm, religion, control. Brick by brick she was walling herself in. She built the walls higher and thicker until they towered above her head and completely surrounded her. Finally I couldn't see her anymore.

Then suddenly a giant iron crowbar began to shatter the walls. Someone very aggressively broke them down blow by blow until they toppled. And behind the rubble was not the woman I'd seen, imposing, confident, sharp-tongued, but a fragile, frightened little girl.

The girl's rescuer tossed down the crowbar, rushed to her, reached down, picked her up out of the debris, and lifted her above His head, smiling and delighted to have freed this beautiful child. It was Jesus. He raised her up in the air, both of them laughing with great joy. He had found her and freed her! Then He wrapped her in His arms and held her close to His chest. He rocked her and nestled His face in her hair. He whispered how much He loved her, how precious she was to Him. He soothed her with His quiet voice. He would not let her go. And she relaxed in His arms.

When Jesus said, "I am the way and the truth and the life" (John 14:6), He meant not only that He was the way to the Father and to heaven, but also that He was the way to freedom and abundant life. He said, "I have come that they may have life, and have it to the full" (John 10:10). He is the way out of every wrong, unjust, and messed-up situation that prevents us from living life to the full. Every sin that we commit, every sin committed against us, every sin that wounds us and keeps us from being fully who He designed us to be…Jesus is the way out.

And when we say that Jesus frees us from sin, we mean not only the acts of sin, but also the *effects* of sin: living in darkness, disease, and the pain of things done to us. We can't speak of salvation through Jesus without recognizing His power to set us free. The prophet Isaiah described the full dimension of the coming Messiah:

The Spirit of the Sovereign Lord is on me, because the
Lord has anointed me to preach good news to the poor.
He has sent me to bind up the brokenhearted, to proclaim
freedom for the captives and release from darkness for the
prisoners, to proclaim the year of the Lord's favor.
ISAIAH 61:1–2

After Jesus read this prophecy in the synagogue, He declared,
"Today this scripture is fulfilled in your hearing" (Luke 4:21). The
New International Version text note says: "Jesus proclaimed libera-
tion from sin and *all its consequences*" (emphasis added).

The Spirit of God knows today, tomorrow…and yesterday. Jesus
knows all the places in our lives that need His healing touch, and His
work at the cross has accomplished the healing we need. Because He
took the sin and pain of our past—*and all its effects*—on Himself,
they no longer have the power to injure us. Paul reminds us:

Now in Christ Jesus you who once were far away have
been brought near through the blood of Christ. For he
himself is our peace, who has made the two one *and has
destroyed the barrier, the dividing wall of hostility,* by abolish-
ing in his flesh the law with its commandments and regu-
lations.… He came and preached peace to you who were
far away and peace to those who were near.
EPHESIANS 2:13–15, 17, EMPHASIS ADDED

"Surely he took up our infirmities and carried our sorrows," said
the prophet Isaiah. "He was pierced for our transgressions, he was
crushed for our iniquities; the punishment that brought us peace was
upon him, and by his wounds we are healed" (Isaiah 53:4–5).

The resurrected Christ now enters the pain of our memories in such power that it actually changes the effect of the past. The purpose of healing is not just to make us feel better. It's to restore us to our original self. It's to set us free from judgment, condemnation, and fear about what others think of us...and the false view we have of ourselves. Jesus overrules the past, transforming our present and our future. And then He calls us to live out of our true personhood—who we really are—in wholeness and freedom.

*Walls protect and walls limit.*
*It is in the nature of walls that they should fall.*—Jeanette Winterson

# REFLECTIONS OF HIS LOVE

Today I heard Loren Johnson's song, and I fell to my knees.

## FOUND

Today—I lost it all
The fences so tall
The well-guarded walls.

Today—I found the breeze
It swept through the trees
And I fell to my knees
I lost what I wanted
Lost what I wanted
Lost what I wanted
Found what I need.

Today—I lost the past
That I held so fast
That nothing could last.

Today—I found the view
The old became new
It led me to You.

Words and music by Loren Johnson,
© 1994 Timmon Music (ASCAP).
From Loren Johnson's album *Simplicity,* 1998, CEO/Monarch Records.
Used by permission.

Lord God,

You know what lies I have believed.

I confess them to You now

and ask You to forgive me for believing them,

including the biggest lie of all: that I don't need a Savior.

Thank You that You have broken down the dividing wall

and destroyed the barrier between us for all of eternity. . .

and for today.

Thank You for coming to shatter the walls

I've built up to protect myself.

Show me any areas in my life where

I still have a brick in my hand.

Heal those areas, Lord,

and keep me from walling myself off from others and from You.

Help me become all that You created me to be.

Chisel away all that needs to be removed from my life.

I trust Your gentle hand.

Amen

# CHAPTER FIVE

# PAST IS PAST

# THE BEAUTY OF SCARS

He redeems my past...

*One thing I do: Forgetting what is behind and straining toward what is ahead, I press on toward the goal to win the prize for which God has called me heavenward in Christ Jesus.—Philippians 3:13–14*

SOMEONE ONCE SAID, "Every woman should know that she can't change the length of her calves, the width of her hips, or the nature of her parents. Her childhood may not have been perfect...but it's over!"

Throughout Scripture, God tells us to "remember...remember...remember." So, yes, sometimes we need to take a look back in order to move into the future that God has planned for us. But we also need to be liberated from the past to live our lives fully and successfully. As devastating as it might have been, the past is just part of our lives. We also have the future...and the present.

"But why did that happen to me?" you may be asking. "Why did I have to go through that?" You may never fully know the answer. But God knows. It was the very thing He used to bring you to where you are right now.

I wouldn't be who I am today if it weren't for what I've gone through in my life. And today I can truly say that I am grateful for the painful things the Lord allowed me to experience, because He has used them to develop things in me that could never have been formed in any other way. If I had been pretty and popular, I might have skated by on my looks. Instead, I had to develop other aspects of myself, like my personality, my intelligence, and my talents. And from my own struggles with rejection and loneliness, I developed empathy and compassion for others who struggle with those feelings.

The things my family went through also shaped me. As I watched my mother and father live their lives, I saw what humility and grace look like and learned that the difficult circumstances of life—however much they may weigh us down or cripple us—don't have to dictate who we become.

Even recent wounds have been unexpected gifts to me. I never really understood the heartache of a woman who desperately wanted to have a child, but couldn't, until it happened to me. My heart could not feel as deeply for families who had lost a child through miscarriage until I experienced that devastating loss too. I didn't really have compassion for actors and others who were struggling with being out of work until I was one of them. In all these trials, God ministered a mercy and tenderness to me that I can now minister to others. And as He has led me into the freedom of forgiving others, I can help others get there too, because I've "been there."

As our wounds become scars, they become more than reminders of what has been—they become reminders of what God has done. We become, as Henry Nouwen calls us, "wounded healers." We have something to give. We are able to dispense God's grace and mercy and healing through the very scars that were once our wounds. What was once damaged is now made whole. What we once hid in shame is now our glory. What was ugly is now beautiful.

When we expose our scars to others, we are saying, "I understand what you've gone through. I understand the pain, the injustice, the betrayal. But look here—take heart! There is One who heals. Your gaping wounds will close too. Only scars will be left."

God has touched the wounds of my past and turned my over-sensitivity to the opinions of others into a deep sensitivity to their needs, so that today I can comfort others with the comfort I've received. With the apostle Paul, I can say:

Praise be to the God and Father of our Lord Jesus Christ,
the Father of compassion and the God of all comfort, who
comforts us in all our troubles, so that we can comfort
those in any trouble with the comfort we ourselves have
received from God.
2 CORINTHIANS 1:3–4

And with Joseph, I can say that what was meant for evil, God meant for good. When God redeems our souls through Christ, He also redeems our pasts. "Everyone is influenced by his or her past," says author and counselor John Trent, "but as Christians, none of us has to be controlled by it."[4] Through the healing of the Holy Spirit of God, we no longer have to be bound by past hurts. We are free to respond to God and to others, to love Him and those around us, from a place of wholeness and acceptance.

No, I wouldn't be who I am today if it weren't for what I've gone through in my life. Neither would you. We've all gone through a lot. But the key is this: We've come through it. And that gives us hope for whatever we're going through today and what we'll be going through tomorrow. God will use whatever we experience for our good, others' healing, and His glory.

*Then Alleluia all my gashes cry!*—*Ruth Pitter*

When Jesus heals the wounds of the past, they lose their power. Serita Ann Jakes reminds us that we should take full advantage of what it means to be born again. Who we are isn't determined by what we've done in the past, and it doesn't depend on what we will do in the future. It is based on our position in Christ.[5] We are a new creation. We are free!

*Deliverance finally comes when you confront*
*your past and put it in its proper perspective.*
*It happened to you but it is not you.*
*You survived the trauma;*
*you too can walk again.*—Serita Ann Jakes

# Out of Egypt

### He delivers me...

*It is for freedom that Christ has set us free.
Stand firm, then, and do not let yourselves be burdened again
by a yoke of slavery.——Galatians 5:1*

THE BOOK OF EXODUS tells us that when the Israelites cried out
to God from their bondage in Egypt, He rescued them. The Lord
spoke to Moses and said,

> "I have indeed seen the misery of my people in Egypt. I
> have heard them crying out because of their slave drivers,
> and I am concerned about their suffering. So I have come
> down to rescue them from the hand of the Egyptians and
> to bring them up out of that land into a good and spa-
> cious land, a land flowing with milk and honey.... So now,
> go. I am sending you to Pharaoh to bring my people the
> Israelites out of Egypt...."
>
> But Moses said to God, "Suppose I go to the Israelites
> and say to them, 'The God of your fathers has sent me to
> you,' and they ask me, 'What is his name?' Then what shall I
> tell them?" God said to Moses, "I AM WHO I AM. This is what
> you are to say to the Israelites: 'I AM has sent me to you.'"
>
> EXODUS 3:7–8, 10, 13–14

"Like the Israelites in captivity, we too are in bondage to an idolatrous culture at odds with the truth—our own Egypt," says pastor Steve Snook. And as He did with the Israelites, God comes to rescue us. He hears our cries, sees our misery, feels our suffering and oppression...and He comes to us. He lifts us up out of captivity in the land of lies and spreads before us a spacious land filled with Himself. He's driven the enemy from our midst, trampled him under His feet, and given us the kingdom. Its beauty takes our breath away. No borders block its vastness. No enemy any longer enslaves us. We spread our arms in freedom. We laugh and dance and play and love. He draws us, and we run together into the fullness of Him.

There has never been a greater symbol of freedom than the Cross. Jesus did what we could not. "A slave can't be set free on his own," says Snook. "Someone has to set him free." First Christ freed us from the law. Now as we abide in Him, He frees us from the bonds of the judgments of others. First He freed us from our own sin. Now He frees us from the emotional residue of the sins committed against us. He frees us from everything we are enslaved to— perfectionism, a performance mentality, the need to control, the "beauty" ideals of the culture, emotions like fear and anger, and addictions of every kind—shopping, food, alcohol, drugs, work, and even exercise.

*free • dom:*
*liberation from slavery or restraint or from the power of another*

Wherever you are in bondage, God brings freedom. "I have seen your misery. I have heard your cry," He said to the Israelites. "I have come to deliver you." And He says it to you. He has delivered you. You have a new name and a new identity. You can say, "I am" because of I

AM. The Son has set us free, and we must grab hold of our liberty, stand squarely in it, and resist the temptation to fall back into old, familiar patterns. As the apostle Paul wrote:

> Under your new Master you're going to experience a marvelous freedom you would never have dreamed of.…
> You…were once held hostage in a sinful society. Then a huge sum was paid out for your ransom. So please don't, out of old habit, slip back into being or doing what everyone else tells you. Friends, stay where you were called to be. God is there. Hold the high ground with him at your side.
>
> 1 CORINTHIANS 7:23, *THE MESSAGE*

When God sets us free, He doesn't just offer freedom from our pasts; He frees us in every area of our lives. Every habit, every sinful attitude, every thought, word, or deed that has kept us imprisoned or paralyzed…He has freed us from them. Let's take the healing we've received and the insights we've gained and move into the future and hope that God has for us.

We've been brought out of Egypt. Let's not go back.

*In the deserts of the heart*
*Let the healing fountain start,*
*In the prison of his days*
*Teach the free man how to praise.—W. H. Auden*

Lord,

thank You that my past is past,

and that You are doing a new thing in me.

Thank You that You have given me a future...and a rich today.

My heart cries out in joy and thanks

for the complete freedom I have in You!

Help me to grasp it with no hesitation, no fear, and no delay.

Help me live in wholeness and freedom all the days of my life

so that You can use me to bring healing to others.

And help me always to remember that

You have brought me out of Egypt,

out of bondage to everything that has ever held me.

I am free! You have said so!

Alleluia!

Amen

CHAPTER SIX

# UNMASKED

# Taking Off the Mask

He takes away the veil...

*Whenever anyone turns to the Lord, the veil is taken away.*——2 *Corinthians* 3:16

ONE HALLOWEEN WHEN I was about twelve or so, I dressed as a 1920s flapper in a dress from the thrift store. I wore yards of pearls for a necklace, feathers in my hair, and a full face mask that looked for all the world like a real face. It was flesh color and translucent, almost see-through, and my own eyes and lips and skin peeked through. It allowed others to see me…but not really. It didn't mask me so much as it morphed me into someone else—someone older, sophisticated, and beautiful.

It was fascinating. The mask looked so natural that you had to look twice to realize it wasn't me. The same thing happened when my friends tried it on: Like magic, the mask conformed to each one's particular bone structure and face shape, obscuring their features, but just ever so slightly. I've often thought about the subtlety of that mask and how many times I've found myself wearing one like it over the years, without ever being consciously aware that I had put it on.

Of course, some of the masks we wear can be as obvious as the faceplate on a suit of armor—like the rage that covers fear, or the arrogance that cloaks insecurity. When you feel ill at ease, do you talk faster or laugh louder, trying to cover your lack of confidence with life-of-the-party bravado? Do you mask feelings of inadequacy with biting wit or sarcasm? How many times do all of us disguise our true feelings behind the safety of a different persona?

Like my Halloween mask, though, some of our disguises are subtler and not so easily discerned, even by ourselves. How often do we hide our sensitive areas behind defensiveness or willfulness, or cover our deep-seated fear with a tyrant's mask of control and invincibility? We're so afraid to be honest—afraid to admit we're hurting, in great need, or in trouble—because we worry about what others might think of us. So we work hard to keep it all together on the surface, to look right on the outside. We hide our fear and pain behind our own plastic mask or painted-on smile.

Maybe we've worn our masks for so many years and they've so conformed to our faces that we don't really know where the masks end and we begin. But God sees the truth, and He asks us to take off our masks and give them to Him. In 2 Corinthians 3:16, Paul reminds us that whenever anyone turns to the Lord, the veil is taken away.

Maybe you're afraid that if others knew all your secrets, they would no longer accept you. Maybe you're even afraid that God might reject you. Are you hiding from Him? You may not even realize that your countless religious activities are really keeping God at arm's length and preventing true intimacy with Him.

You're not fooling anyone. You may think that no one notices, but others can see the look of emptiness, loneliness, and loss in your eyes. They notice the weight you've gained or lost in your attempt to fill the void. They know that you've been hiding and avoiding relationships. And you're not fooling God. He already knows everything about you.

Why are we so afraid of being honest with God? He already

knows every secret we harbor, even the ones we don't know we have…yet He never leaves us. He already knows our lies and our weaknesses and our disobedience…yet He never leaves us. While others may never have taken the time to find out what we think or how we feel, He knows. We don't have to go to emotional extremes just to get His attention, and we don't have to pretend we don't have any needs. So why are we so afraid of being honest with God?

The beauty of God is that you no longer have to pretend. He wants you to come to Him just as you are. You don't have to "be" anyone else. He's not angry or offended by the things you've done to mask your pain. His heart breaks over the cruel, unjust things that have been done to you. He knows the rejection you've suffered. He knows the abuse and indignities that have scarred you. He knows the things you lived through at age eight and ten and fourteen…and forty. He knows.

God holds the crowbar to dismantle your wall and the key to unlock your cage. He's waiting to come in and rescue you. He's just waiting for you to say yes. He won't force Himself on you, but He's patiently waiting for you to give Him your pain, your past, your fear, your need…and your mask.

Let honesty come. It's nothing to fear; it's the beginning of free-dom—for yourself, for the ones you love, for your dreams. Do you see His arms? They're open to you. So just as King David cried out, let us "run together into the fullness of Him!"

*Man is born broken. He lives by mending.*
*The grace of God is glue.—Eugene O'Neill*

# AN IDENTITY CRISIS

He will never forsake me...

*Though my father and mother forsake me,*
*the Lord will receive me.——Psalm 27:10*

IT'S HARD TO BREAK out of the familiar, even when it's crippling us. We're bound by actions and reactions that we don't even like, but we're apprehensive about changing them. We don't want to rock the boat; we don't want to upset people.

We're afraid of what we might "lose" if we get real, not realizing what we've already lost by settling for the counterfeit. We're not sure how others will respond to us. We could be rejected. Misunderstood. Disliked. Worst of all, alone. We could alienate the people around us. Then what? Okay, so we may not like all the dynamics in our relationships—maybe they're not so healthy—but at least they're familiar. We know what to expect.

Just ask my friend Jamie.

For years, Jamie's parents and siblings used her to transmit messages to one another. She was always in the middle of sibling squabbles and family misunderstandings. This one was mad at that one, and what did he say about her, and you tell Mom we're not coming if brother is there. The youngest in a family of dominant personalities, Jamie could never stand up to her family and tell them to leave her out of their soap operas, so she placated everyone as best she could.

Change came once Jamie took off her mask. She had been so enmeshed in her situation that she hadn't really known how crazy it was and how she herself contributed to the family dynamic. As she began to get real in her own life, she realized how much of her identity was wrapped up in her role as peacemaker. It made her feel important. In her need for approval, she enjoyed the part of the "good daughter" and the subtle kind of power it gave her with her parents. She enjoyed the feeling of superiority. But sadly, she also began to realize that her relationship with her siblings was based only upon her role as messenger.

Jamie finally began to tell her family that she didn't want to be in that position anymore. She took off the mask that she'd worn for so long. It wasn't easy, because she had become addicted to the drama and constant crisis, and for a while she was punished with silence from some members of her family and outrage from others. But she stuck to her guns, and as she began to understand how she had used the situation to meet her own needs, she began to understand her family's needs and hurts too.

As her own mask came off, Jamie began to see through the masks the other family members wore. She saw how they too were covering their insecurities and hurts behind their own facades. She began to see them with new eyes—eyes of compassion—and she began to understand them better and how to relate to them as they really were.

After a while Jamie's family began to talk with one another without her in the middle. Now an entire family is changing for the better because one person decided to get real.

# I WANNA BE ME...I THINK

He calls me by a new name...

*You will be called by a new name*
*that the mouth of the Lord will bestow.——Isaiah 62:2*

"I WANNA BE ME," we warble along with Frank Sinatra. But
sometimes that's the last thing we really want to be. It's too risky. We
say we want to be accepted for who we really are, but there's so much
uncertainty.

I have a confession: I desperately long to be known for who I
really am, yet I'm also terrified of it. If we're really honest, there's a
part of each of us that lives in a vague sort of fear that one day we'll
be discovered for who we really are and everyone will be horrified.

My four-year-old goddaughter has found the formula. She's discovered that her little bumblebee song wins her the attention and
acceptance of all the people in the room. When she sings it, they are
enthralled. So she sings it over and over and over again.

*Thea was still under the belief that...*
*if you clucked often enough,*
*the hens would mistake you*
*for one of themselves.——Willa Cather*

I realize that I'm a lot like my little goddaughter. Like a four-year-old, I sometimes still think I have to keep doing something to win people's acceptance. Many of us define ourselves by how others react to us. In *The Sacred Romance*, Brent Curtis and John Eldredge write that our identity is *bestowed:* We are who we are in relation to others. We draw our identities from *how* and *if* we impact others.[6]

They go on to say that if failing draws attention, we will become failures; if performing brings acceptance, we will become performers. The used and abused will become victims; the nobodies will fade away; the somebodies will do whatever it is that made them feel like somebody. And once we find something that brings us attention or affirmation, we have to keep doing it—again and again and again—to maintain our identity.

> *There is no escaping your identity.*
> *You will not live beyond how you see yourself;*
> *not for long.—Brent Curtis and John Eldredge*

In *Telling Secrets*, Frederick Buechner says:

Because we have to survive after all, we try to make ourselves into something that we hope the world will like better than it apparently did the selves we originally were…and in the process…our shimmering self gets buried so deep that most of us hardly end up living out of it at all. Instead, we live out all the other selves which we are constantly putting on and taking off like coats and hats against the world's weather.[7]

And the weather, as the song says, "is frightful." But the fire of God's love is so delightful! It warms us and illuminates the way to our true identity.

If it's true that you draw your identity from how you impact others, you need to be reminded of how powerfully you've impacted God. Look at His enormous love for you! Look at what He did: He gave His own Son for you! He gave you His own identity. He made you a new creation and changed your name, so that you can glorify His.

You are *loved;* you didn't earn it and you can't lose it. It's God's gift to you. He has freed you to be yourself, to grow up inside yourself in the power of the risen Lord and to go forth in wholeness and freedom to fulfill your purpose and destiny.[8]

*The shortest and surest way to live with honor*
*in the world is to be in reality what we*
*would appear to be.—Socrates*

Father,

help me to take off my mask.

Help me to slip my hand in Yours

and yield the parts of myself I've protected so carefully.

Thank You that I don't have to be anyone

but who You created me to be.

Help me discover who that is.

I give you access, Holy Spirit.

Show me my true identity—all that I am in You.

Give me the courage to change those things

that keep me from being real.

Thank You that You accept me as I am

and that You will never leave me.

Help me every day, Lord, to become more of the authentic,

beautiful woman You created me to be.

I eagerly look forward to discovering who I really am!

Amen

# CHAPTER SEVEN

# GREAT
# EXPECTATIONS

# I Don't Believe I've Met You

I am chosen...

*You do not belong to the world,*
*but I have chosen you out of the world.*——John 15:19

Is there someone you're always trying to meet? Like other people's expectations?

"Oh, hello, I don't believe we've met."

"I'm other people's expectations."

"Oh, is that right? No, I've never been able to meet you!"

Ever try to meet everybody's expectations? I have. Whew! It's exhausting! And you know, no matter how hard you try, somehow you never really succeed at it anyway.

I'm an actress, but I'm also a pastor's wife. So sometimes I can feel a bit schizophrenic. I've sometimes assumed that I *should* be a certain way—more attractive, less attractive, more scholarly, less lively, and so on, depending on which role I was filling at the time. As an actress, I'm accustomed to people expecting me to always be gorgeous and sparkling. But as a pastor's wife, I thought I should go out of my way to do the opposite—not to laugh so loud or talk so much, and definitely dress down to deflect attention from myself. I didn't wear much makeup or really do my hair. I kept myself very natural, even doing less than I normally would for my daily life, I suppose because I was afraid that it would seem like I was trying to grab the spotlight.

A few years ago a couple of the church ministry staff reprimanded me. "Don't shrink back," they said. "Don't diminish yourself. Don't try to undo how God has made you. You don't even realize that when you walk in the beauty that God has given you, you minister to other people."

I didn't understand quite what they meant. I told them I had been afraid people would think I was being showy.

"Do you do it to be showy?" they asked.

"No. I do it to be my best," I replied.

"Then don't worry about it," they said. "God has anointed that in you. We may not even recognize an anointing. Combining the things He gave you naturally, innately, with the things you can do to enhance what He's given you is the very thing He uses to encourage other women. You don't know what the power of that ministry is. And it gives women freedom to be who they are and to become their best too."

I felt released. And I felt that it was the truth. When we are our best, either in appearance or attitude or spirit, we just feel better. After all, our appearance simply reflects who we are on the inside. Real, authentic beauty doesn't reside on the surface; it emanates from within.

So don't shrink back! You are free to be who God created you to be. That's what He can use; that's what He loves. That honors Him.

*Am I a prisoner of people's expectations, or liberated by Divine promises?—Henri Nouwen*

✺

# REFLECTIONS OF HIS LOVE

As I meditated on what my friends at church had said to me, I felt the Lord Himself speak to my heart about it:

"I need you to move forward, not retreat. I make each one individual and special. I made you vibrant to make a difference, to take a stand. But you worry about others liking you, your husband approving of you. Don't worry about that. I love you. I delight in your personality. I made you to flourish and stand out! I designed it! Enjoy! That's what I can use, not the shrinking violet or wallflower. You don't realize it, but that's dishonoring to Me. What others would give to have all and be all that I made you! You have the power to bless people; don't withhold it from them. And it's not just being "nice"; it's speaking the truth to them, and just being yourself in their presence. Don't worry about going too far or being a spectacle or overbearing: I'll rein you in. This will not be exhausting—it will be liberating. You'll be free!"

# The Girl with the Curl

## I am His own...

*For the sake of his great name the Lord will not reject his people, because the Lord was pleased to make you his own.*——1 Samuel 12:22

Do you remember learning this nursery rhyme when you were young?

> There was a little girl who had a little curl,
> Right in the middle of her forehead.
> And when she was good, she was very, very good,
> But when she was bad, she was horrid.

In *When the Heart Waits,* Sue Monk Kidd says that it sends a powerful message to girls:

> Personify the good side of the little girl: smile sweetly, be pleasing, do what's expected—no straying outside the lines. Suppress the mind-of-your-own dimension, which tends to sour everyone. As adult "good girls," that means be pleasant, compliant, and sweet and "nice." Get what you want or need through charm, not directness. Be cool as a cucumber and poised as can be on the outside, regard-less of the chaos on the inside.[9]

"In other words," Kidd says, "when it comes to life, keep every hair in place."

How many of us are still living out that nursery rhyme from our childhood? We pretend to be happy and put on a happy face even when we feel like crying. We find ourselves trying hard to fit in with a group when we don't really care that much about them to begin with. We pretend to be something we aren't because we know that's what people expect of us.

Does that sound like you? Does every hair have to be in place?

If you do these kinds of things, you're telling yourself the worst possible lie. In essence, says Dr. Kevin Leman, you're saying that your real self isn't good enough, that who you really are doesn't measure up, that you're just not acceptable as you are…so you have to put on a false face. And if you're really good at it you can fool just about everybody…except yourself.[10]

*Who in the world am I?*
*Ah, that's the great puzzle.* —Lewis Carroll

Deep down you know you're pretending, and your charade just further erodes your self-esteem. What if people *do* like you or affirm you or accept you? You know that it's not the "real you" they're responding to at all, and you become even more insecure about how they would receive the real you. And then you become paranoid about keeping up the facade, because sooner or later the truth might come out and people would see you for who you really are.

Does this sound like you? Do you find yourself struggling with trying to be someone else? Do you find yourself saying yes when you mean no and no when you mean yes? Do you find yourself being with people and doing things that don't really feel right for you?

It's an exhausting way to live, isn't it? But what you don't realize is that people would like you every bit as much—probably even more—if they could see the real you.

The first step toward your real self is to be honest—with God, with yourself, and with others. It doesn't happen in one day, but it does happen little by little as you become totally honest with yourself. If you don't, you'll just stay on the merry-go-round of lies.

In *How to Raise Your Self-Esteem*, Dr. Nathaniel Branden suggests a written exercise for becoming honest and getting to know the real you. Fill in the blank to complete this sentence: "I like myself least when I _____." He says to add everything you can think of and to be brutally honest. Then do the same thing with "I like myself most when _____." When you start thinking about what you like and don't like, who you are and who you aren't, you start to see your own actions and motivations more clearly. Then you can begin to discover the real you and stop doing things that are self-defeating.[11]

Therapist Charlene Johnson uses a similar technique. She had me make a list of what I believed I had to be in order to be "acceptable." I was to fill in the blank: "I am a good girl if _____." Being the perfectionistic/people pleasing/compliant person that I'd been all my life, my list was pretty long. Seemed like it took a whole legal pad. Not just a page of the pad—the whole thing! I won't tell you everything on my list—it's too scary!—but we might have a few similarities. I believe I'm a "good" girl if:

- I please everyone around me;
- I'm responsible;
- I don't need others' help;
- I don't upset my friends;
- I'm articulate and don't embarrass my husband;

&#8463; I make my home beautiful;

&#8463; I do everything I'm expected to do;

&#8463; I do everything I'm asked to do.

It wasn't that some of these things—like making my home lovely and staying organized—weren't valid desires; the problem was my *need* to do them in order to feel valued and accepted and "good." That was the lie.

After I did that exercise, I was instructed to go back through the lies one by one and renounce each one before the Lord. Then I asked Him to heal that place in me, that need, that believed the lies. And then I asked Him to replace the lies with the truth of who I was to be.

The real way to overcome the lies of the enemy is with the truth of God. Write down the lie. What is the lie that I believe about myself? What is the judgment I've made against myself that's keeping me from loving and enjoying God and being a full participant in His Kingdom? What is it? Write out the lie. Expose it, confess it, repent of it, and renounce it.

*Expose it:* I understand that believing I have no value is a lie.

*Confess it:* Lord, I confess I have sinned by believing this lie.

*Repent of it:* I turn around. I'm not going to believe it anymore.

*Renounce it:* In Jesus' name, I break its power over me.

If that was the lie, what's the truth about me? Pray: *Lord, fill in this lie with Your truth. I am accepted, I am loved, I am Your own, I am precious to You, I do have a future....*

Continually renew your mind with Scriptures that tell you who you are in Christ. Use the list in the back of this book. Memorize the verses. Believe them. Speak them aloud to yourself and pray them back to God with gratitude.

As it was with the lie you believed, so it is with the truth. God's truth displaces the lie. Let the power of that truth rule your heart and mind now, and your faith will grow as you exercise it. And the Bible promises: "The mind controlled by the Spirit is life and peace" (Romans 8:6).

It's freeing to realize that you don't have to be what everyone else expects you to be, or even what you expect yourself to be. You have only to be who you really are. That's who God expects you to be.

And every hair doesn't have to be in place.

*It's never too late to be what you might have been.—George Eliot*

Lord,

I thank You for setting me free—

from sin, from lies, from the expectations of others,

and from bondage to the culture that surrounds me.

When You chose me in eternity past,

and then knit me together in my mother's womb,

You planned to use me just as You made me.

It is enough for You—so it is enough for me.

Thank You that I don't have to pretend

or try to be someone else.

Help me to remember every day who I am in Christ.

And help me to remember that I honor You

by being all that You created me to be.

Amen

# CHAPTER EIGHT

# PURSUED BY LOVE

# Drawn to Love

He loves me with an everlasting love...

*"I have loved you with an everlasting love;
I have drawn you with loving-kindness." —Jeremiah 31:3*

Josh first noticed Janet at the coffee bar. They both got their first cup of the day there several times a week. Josh always timed his cappuccino visits to coincide with Janet's lattes. Every time he saw her he smiled, asked how she was doing, and commented on the weather or her pretty outfit. Janet never noticed. He might as well have been invisible. Janet was interested in guys with more charisma.

Three weeks went by. Then one day Janet spilled coffee all over the counter. When Josh helped her clean it up, she saw him for the first time. They talked for a few minutes as they licked foam from their drinks. He invited her on a date, but she turned him down. More weeks went by, and Josh kept smiling, asking, and hoping.

A few months later I was visiting Janet at her home when her phone rang. She let the answering machine pick up. "I bet it's him again," she sighed, a bit impatiently. "You gotta hear this."

"Oh, hi, Janet. It's Josh. Just wanted to say hello. It's a beautiful day outside—it made me think of you. I was hoping I could take you out for lunch. Well, you're not there. I'll keep trying. Bye."

"That's the third phone call this week!" Janet exclaimed.

"He sounds nice," I said. "Why won't you go out with him?"

"He's not my type," she replied. "Not exciting—not romantic enough."

I wasn't surprised that Janet couldn't see Josh. She was too distracted by the razzmatazz types to notice him. But Josh didn't give up. He faithfully pursued her: He brought her flowers, wrote her love letters and poems, and even sang her songs. Slowly, slowly Janet's eyes were opened, until one day she finally saw him for who he was: faithful, kind, loving...and wildly romantic.

That's how God pursues us. He initiates and pursues a love relationship with us long before we're interested—while, in fact, we're running from Him. Simon Tugwell wrote:

> Very often we are not looking for God; far from it, we are in
> full flight from him, in high rebellion against him. And he
> knows that.... He has followed us into our own darkness;
> there where we thought finally to escape him, we run straight
> into his arms. So we do not have to erect a false piety for our-
> selves, to give us the hope of salvation. Our hope is in his
> determination to save us, and he will not give in.[12]

It was God's relentless, loving pursuit of me that brought me running straight into His arms on that beach in Hawaii. Suddenly I had the stark realization that He died on the cross for *me*. I'd known that before, of course, but now the knowing moved from my head to my heart. I finally understood in my deepest being what a powerful demonstration of love this was and what Paul meant when he wrote: "God demonstrates his own love for us in this: While we were still sinners, Christ died for us" (Romans 5:8).

I love how Brennan Manning describes his own encounter with Christ and how it changed him forever:

Without warning I felt a hand grip my heart. I could hardly breathe. The awareness of being loved was no longer gentle, tender, and comfortable. The love of Christ, the crucified Son of God for me, took on the wildness and the passion, the fury of a sudden storm in springtime. Spasms of convulsive crying erupted from the depths of my being. He died on the cross for me. I'd known that before. I'd heard it in grade school, church, from the priests, the nuns. But I knew it in a way that you might call notional knowledge, just another trinket in the pawnshop of my doctrinal beliefs. Now in one blinding moment it was real knowledge, calling for personal engagement of my mind and my heart. Christianity was no longer simply a moral code or an ethic or a philosophy of life, but a love affair—the thrill, the excitement, the incredible passionate joy of being loved unconditionally and falling in love with Jesus.[13]

Knowing such a love will change us. But we must allow ourselves to *be* loved. It's about entering God's presence and allowing His Spirit to enter us. "It's in relationship that we learn to love," write Dr. Henry Cloud and Dr. John Townsend. "We receive love, and this teaches us how to love. We love 'because He first loved us' (1 John 4:19)."[14] Then, when we give to others out of that abundant love we've received, there is no end to its miraculous supply.

Jesus pursues us from the start. When we are lost, He comes looking for us. The lover of our soul knocks on the door of our hearts, and when we answer, He comes in and lavishes love, abundant life, and even all of eternity on us. We love Him *only* because He first loved us.

# ROOTED IN LOVE

I belong to Him…

*I belong to my lover,*
*and his desire is for me.* —Song of Songs 7:10

SOMEONE ONCE SAID, "You wouldn't be so worried about what others thought of you if you realized how seldom they do." But there is Someone who thinks about you constantly…and wants to love you into being.

Why does Jesus want to do this? Because He *is* love. Sadly, very few of us seem to have a deep revelation of how much God loves us. Yes, we know that His love is there, but it's not *real* to us, so it doesn't change us as it should. But Paul's prayer for the church at Ephesus clearly states that being rooted in God's love is what we need most:

May Christ through your faith [actually] dwell—settle down, abide, make His permanent home—in your hearts! May you be rooted deep in love and founded securely on love. That you may have the power and be strong to apprehend and grasp with all the saints (God's devoted people, the experience of that love) what is the breadth and length and height and depth [of it]. [That you may really come] to know—practically, through experience for

yourselves—the love of Christ, which far surpasses mere
knowledge (without experience). That you may be filled
(through all your being) unto all the fullness of God—
[that is] may have the richest measure of the divine
Presence, and become a body wholly filled and flooded
with God Himself!

EPHESIANS 3:17–19, AMP

In *The Message,* a contemporary language version of the Bible,
this passage says:

I ask him to strengthen you by his Spirit—not a brute
strength but a glorious inner strength—that Christ will
live in you as you open the door and invite him in. And I
ask him that with both feet planted firmly on love, you'll
be able to take in with all Christians the extravagant
dimensions of Christ's love. Reach out and experience the
breadth! Test its length! Plumb the depths! Rise to the
heights! Live full lives, full in the fullness of God. God can
do anything, you know—far more than you could ever
imagine or guess or request in your wildest dreams! He
does it not by pushing us around but by working within
us, his Spirit deeply and gently within us.

Paul could have prayed for the Ephesian believers to have the
power to perform miracles or to exercise authority over Satan.
Instead, he prayed for the church to be rooted in God's love, because
He knew that was the source from which everything else would flow.

Clearly, God knows that we need to *experience* His love—to have
not just a head knowledge, but a deep revelation that makes us secure
in His presence and gives us the courage to let down the walls and

let go of our old ways of defending and protecting ourselves. The Lord delights in you! His desire is for you! You are His beloved, and what He wants more than anything else is deep, intimate relationship with you so He can show you how very much He loves you.

Thomas Merton's peers once said to him: "You've published many books; you're one of the most famous spiritual men in the world; kings and presidents seek after you. Who are you?"

Without hesitation, Merton replied, "The deepest awareness that I have of myself is that I am a man passionately loved by Jesus Christ."

When we grasp the perfect, complete love God has for us, fear loses its grip on our lives. Perfect love casts out fear. When we have a true revelation of how much God loves us, we are free. Neither Satan, nor your past, nor the opinions of others, nor your own insecurities can shake the awareness at your core that you know you are loved, no matter what. The Bible assures us that nothing can ever take that away:

> For I am convinced that neither death nor life, neither
> angels nor demons, neither the present nor the future, nor
> any powers, neither height nor depth, nor anything else in
> all creation, will be able to separate us from the love of
> God that is in Christ Jesus our Lord.
>
> ROMANS 8:38–39

When we fully grasp that, says Brennan Manning, a life of "affections, awe, spontaneous praise and profound wonder results."[15]

# REFLECTIONS OF HIS LOVE

Today feeling overwhelmed and blue, fat, undisciplined, intentionally going in every direction except the one I should. Instead of going to the gym or for a run, or quieting myself before God, I was standing in the checkout line at the grocery store with cheese, crackers, pâté, and a Snickers bar. And God invaded my mind: "Where can you hide from My love?" It pierced my heart.

Even in my weakness and lack of resolve, even though I dislike myself right now, He comes after me. But the biggest surprise is that He comes not with discipline, not with condemnation—He knows the times when we have self-imposed enough of that, I guess. Instead, He meets me with love and affection.

His hot pursuit is not to reproach or scold, but to bring affection and tenderness. It blew over me like a cool breeze. It was an epiphany. I was indeed running and hiding from Him, but instead of reprimand, a reminder: He was pursuing me to love me, to take me closer into Himself, to draw me in. And like a squirming two-year-old, I was scrambling to get down off His lap.

Then He reminded me of a love letter He wrote: "Arise, my darling, my beautiful one, and come with me. See! The winter is past; the rains are over and gone. Flowers appear on the earth; the season of singing has come" (Song of Songs 2:10–12).

I left my groceries at the store and left with Him....

# Magnificent Obsession

He is enthralled with me...

*The king is enthralled by your beauty;*
*honor him, for he is your lord.—Psalm 45:11*

WALKING ALONG RODEO Drive to meet a friend for coffee, I saw
two women greet each other.

"Gosh, you are so *skinny!*" said the first.

"Really? Thanks!" The second one beamed in total delight.

It struck me. Why was a remark like that taken as an automatic
compliment? Maybe it's just in Beverly Hills.

But maybe not.

I think at one time or another most of us obsess about being
thin. I have to raise my own hand here—guilty. Those pesky television cameras add ten pounds, so I try to stay slimmer than I would
if I didn't have to live my life "on camera." I agree with actress Kitty
Carlisle, who said, "TV cameras seem to add ten pounds to me. So
I make it a policy never to eat TV cameras."

Nonetheless, staying slender is not always easy—especially when
you're over forty. I have to confess that when I meet someone who
says, "Oh, you look so much thinner in real life," I like it...but I also
cringe. I get a momentary ego fluff and then wonder *Hmm.... Does*

*that mean millions of viewers think I look heavy? Oh no! Maybe I should lose five pounds. Or ten!*

I obsess. Even if it's just for a moment. Or an hour. Or a week.

*If American men are obsessed with money, American women are obsessed with weight. The men talk of gain, the women talk of loss, and I do not know which talk is the more boring.*—Marya Mannes

I'm not saying that we shouldn't be concerned about our weight. We all know that excess weight can lead to health problems. I'm talking about the unrealistic expectation that we should look like we've just sprung off the pages of a fashion magazine, even when the circumstances of our lives, our body type, or our age dictate otherwise.

In the obsession with being skinny, many women today have forgotten that the aim should be to maintain long-term quality of life that's measured by energy and vitality, not by dress size and the number on the scale.

We are sacrificing our identities, our health—and even our lives—by embracing starvation diets, exercising fanatically, or gobbling little herbal accelerator pills or funny liquid drinks. And as we fixate on having to look a certain way, we fail to appreciate the one-of-a-kind individuals we truly are.

Remember: Christ bought your identity. He has freed you from the tyranny of other people's expectations and unshackled you from the bonds of comparisons. Your identity isn't determined by *Vogue* magazine, Victoria's Secret, or Calvin Klein, and you don't have to try to meet the unreasonable, unattainable standards of the culture. You are unique in every way. So resist the idea of living someone else's idea of what you should look like.

The truth is that when we do that, our real obsession is our preoccupation with ourselves. When we strive to be skinny, we ourselves dominate our thoughts. In our distraction, we often don't lavish time and attention on loved ones, the people around us, or God. We fixate on and spend our passions on ourselves. And even if we despise them, our bodies become the focus of our attention, idols we worship—our own *golden calves*. But God says that He will not share His glory with idols. "On that day, I will banish the names of the idols from the land, and they will be remembered no more" (Zechariah 13:2).

When we obsess about being skinny, we not only worship a false god, but we also often miss what is truly meaningful and beautiful. That became clear to me when I met my friend a few steps farther down Rodeo Drive.

Her model-thin body had changed some since the birth of her daughter two years earlier. She was rounder and softer. The corner of a finger painting peeked out of her bag, and her shoes were covered with sand from the playground. Last season's clothes bore the telltale smudge of a cherry Popsicle. I was struck—by her absolute beauty.

My friend lamented the loss of her size-six figure only briefly. With a shrug of her lovely shoulders and a smile that spoke volumes about her deep contentment, she said, "Oh, I've quit obsessing about it." And then, beaming, she added, "Wait till you meet my little girl!"

That's how God feels about us! We are His obsession, and He should be ours. The more we direct our attention to Him and the more we satisfy our hunger with Him, the more obsessed with His goodness and majesty we become. And we find that as we focus on Him, He changes our desires and priorities. What we once obsessed about seems insignificant in the light of His nature and truth, and He becomes our magnificent obsession.

Father God,

Thank You for working deeply and gently within me

to draw me to Yourself. Enlarge my heart, O God.

Expand my capacity to love You...and to receive Your love.

Help me to grasp the life-changing truth

that You love me with an everlasting love!

I confess to You all the thoughts, passions,

and desires of my heart that are not from You.

Forgive me for giving myself center stage

and making me the object of my attention.

I want to make You my magnificent obsession.

I want to be enthralled by nothing but You.

Thank You that I am Your beloved...

and that You are mine.

Amen

# CHAPTER NINE

# A FAMILY RESEMBLANCE

# A Rich Inheritance

He gives me the riches of His inheritance...

*I pray also that . . . you may know the hope to which he has called you, the riches of his glorious inheritance in the saints.*——*Ephesians 1:18*

FAMILY RESEMBLANCE IS amazing. Growing up, I knew a family with four sons. All of them, including their parents and grand-parents, had an identical walk. You could spot them in a crowd and put them together even if you never saw their faces. My friend Sally's daughters have her gorgeous skin, and my husband, Larry, has his mother's perfect nose. My cousin Laura's daughter, Sarah, has her same charming, crooked little smile and soft voice. Another cousin, Frank, has his father's receding jaw...and matching hairline.

What physical traits did you inherit from your family? I can tell you that I inherited my mother's eye shape and my dad's eye color. I also got my dad's cleft chin, the Stafford body build and slim legs, and, oh yes, their lousy vision. Some say that my eyes are pretty, but I have to tell you: They're strictly for looks.

From my mom and her mother I got my height—all three of us are five feet nine inches tall—along with, oh joy, the famed Langley derriere. I always figured we needed the extra height as a counter-balance. My grandmother, "Bombo," (the first grandchild's two-year-old attempt at "Grandma") used to say, almost proudly as she shook her head with a smile, "None of us Langley women are scarce-hipped." I'm not scarce-hipped either.

*I had to face the facts: I was pear-shaped. I was a bit depressed because I hate pears. 'Specially their shape.*—Charlotte Bingham

While I have to admit that it's not my favorite family trait, it's a small price to pay for being a Langley. Because from Bombo I also inherited long, tapered fingers for playing the piano, her love for writing, and the legacy of a deep personal faith. If I can have my mom's hospitality and creativity, I'll gladly endure the Langley freckles and backside. And for my dad's inner strength and humility, I'll welcome the Stafford poor vision and high cholesterol. My mother's tenderness, humor, and optimism, and my daddy's integrity, faithfulness, and courage are traits I pray I will exhibit more and more as the years pass.

Our DNA is rich. We are the recipients of the best, sometimes the worst, always the most surprising aspects of our family history—all arranged in a unique package that has never appeared before and never will again. As you look at what you've inherited from your family, I'm sure you'll find more to celebrate than to scorn.

*He who remembers the benefits of his parents is too much occupied with his recollections to remember their faults.*—Pierre Jean Beranger

And that's just your natural inheritance. Take some time to think about your spiritual inheritance, and you'll be blown away. Because you're a joint heir with Christ, you have an imperishable inheritance:

- ☞ You've received the gift of righteousness through the shed blood of Jesus.
- ☞ You've received deliverance from the power of darkness and been brought into the kingdom of God.
- ☞ You've received healing by the stripes of Jesus.
- ☞ You've received strength with all might according to His glorious power.
- ☞ You've received the spirit of wisdom and revelation in the knowledge of Him.
- ☞ You've received the peace of God that passes understanding.
- ☞ You've received the mind of Christ.
- ☞ You've received the power of the Holy Spirit.

Yes, I can see that you do have a family resemblance—you reflect the image of your mother and father. But even more, because of Jesus, you reflect the image of God. It's no wonder you have a family resemblance. You're a daughter of the King!

*If gratitude is due from children to their earthly parent, how much more is the gratitude of the great family of men due to our father in heaven.*—Hosea Ballou

# ABOUNDING IN THANKSGIVING

He fills me with thankfulness…

*As you received Christ Jesus as Lord, continue to live in him…overflowing with thankfulness.—Colossians 2:6–7*

IN "TWO-HEADED WOMAN," Lucille Clifton has some pretty amazing things to say about hips:[16]

> These hips are big hips
> They don't like to be held back
> These hips have never been enslaved
> They go where they want to go
> They do what they want to do
> These hips are mighty hips
> These hips are magic hips.

Wow! Is that the way you feel about your hips? Your arms? Do you embrace and accept the beauty and power of your body with gratitude and thanksgiving? No? Then let's change that. Let's start to change the way we think—and talk—about ourselves.

We've been changed; we've put off the old stuff. As the Living Bible puts it, we're "living a brand new kind of life that is continually learning more and more of what is right" (Colossians 3:10, TLB).

Jesus is showing us more and more of who He is and who we are. Let's let Him change our thinking too.

*Every year of my life I grow more convinced that it is wisest and best to fix our attention on the beautiful and the good, and dwell as little as possible on the evil and the false.*—Richard Cecil

We mustn't underestimate the importance of our thought life in how we feel about ourselves. That's why Paul wrote down this reminder: "Whatever is true, whatever is noble, whatever is right, whatever is pure, whatever is lovely, whatever is admirable—if anything is excellent or praiseworthy—think about such things" (Philippians 4:8). No, I'm not advocating some New Age philosophy of positive thinking or self-realization. No superficial "You are great!" affirmations in the mirror every morning. But I do believe that if we think of ourselves as fat, ugly, hopeless-so-why-bother, we condemn our bodies with our words. In our disappointment and disdain, we can't help but treat our bodies disrespectfully, and our words become self-fulfilling prophecies.

But when we view ourselves—including our bodies—with love and acceptance, when we have a healthy view of the love God has for us just as we are, we can begin to nurture our bodies and treat them as allies instead of adversaries.

*Until you make peace with who you are, you'll never be content with what you have.*—Doris Mortman

When you look at your hips, instead of just seeing those extra inches you can pinch, or wistfully comparing their width to a twenty-something model in a magazine, stop…and look at them with new eyes.

Look at those hips! They help you give birth to babies, and your children straddle them the first years of their lives. Your hips help you stand firm for what is right, and you plant your hands on them in righteous indignation over what is wrong. Your hips endure torturous aluminum benches at soccer matches and dance the night away at birthday parties. Your hips bring such life and joy!

Look at those arms! When you wave good-bye and feel the jiggle of your soft upper arms, don't disparage them as "granny bye-bye" arms. Be grateful for that mother or grandmother in your life, whose exuberant waves welcomed you home and sent you on your way again back into the world. Those arms carry everything from babies to briefcases. They wrestle with everything from groceries to gurneys. They push lawnmowers and wheelchairs and five-year-olds on swings. They lovingly hold your frightened German shepherd puppy. They tenderly hug your elderly mother, and they playfully encircle the neck of your husband. And soon, they'll be waving "granny bye-byes" at the doorstep to grown-ups who will cherish every memory of your every embrace.

If you ask me, I've never seen more beautiful arms and hips!

*The body is a sacred garment. It's your first and last garment;*
*it is what you enter life in and what you depart life with,*
*and it should be treated with honor.* — Martha Graham

# LEAVING A LEGACY

I will pass on an inheritance…

*Be careful to follow all the commands of the Lord your God,
that you may possess this good land and pass it on as an inheritance
to your descendants forever.——1 Chronicles 28:8*

YOU HAVE RECEIVED an incredible inheritance. Now, what will you pass on to your children? What legacy will you leave them? No, I'm not talking about real estate or a living trust or an insurance policy. I'm not even talking about raising your children to love God or training them in the way they should go. I'm talking about something else we pass down: Just like brown hair or artistic ability, self-loathing is often hereditary.

My friend Sandy says that as a little girl she learned to hate her body from being around people who hated theirs. Hating our bodies is a learned behavior, sort of like driving or spelling or table manners, and we can pass down our obsession with our imperfect selves to our children and others we influence. We need to resist putting ourselves down.

Talking negatively about our bodies can actually lead us—and those around us—to obsess about our looks. How do you talk about yourself around your children? How much emphasis do you put on your appearance or weight, and how much energy is centered on your looks? Do you place an extremely high premium on your appearance and expect your daughter to do the same?

Be aware of how your attitude about food and dieting affects your daughter and others close to you. They're watching you. If you freak out when you gain a few pounds, they will too. If you allow emotions to guide your eating—if you starve or stuff yourself—they will too.

*Self-love is the only weight-loss aid*
*that really works in the long run.*—*Jenny Craig*

Recognize if you are putting pressure on your child to look good or to lose weight. Do you use food as either a reward or a punishment in your family? Do you frequently comment on your daughter's appearance—her clothes, makeup, hair? Do you view her appearance as reflecting either negatively or positively on you?

The good news is that the legacy of false self-perception and grasping for impossible images can end with us. We don't have to pass down our self-loathing or our obsessions. Because we are in Christ, we've been radically changed. We're no longer slaves to the standards or hostage to the values of this world.

It's not easy to resist the media messages that bombard us, but we must. Most of us have accepted society's standards of beauty, no questions asked, even though these standards often undermine our self-image, our self-worth, our physical—and certainly our spiritual—well-being. Let's not bow our knee to the idols of our age. Let's be radically countercultural!

We can break free...and take some captives with us. In our own spheres of influence—with our children, sisters, mothers, friends, and coworkers—we have the power to either perpetuate the culture's attitude or overcome it. We can possess this land, carrying the truth, and do our best to pass it on as an inheritance to our descendants forever.

*A good man leaves an inheritance
for his children's children.——Proverbs 13:22*

Sandy has come a long way in making peace with the body she learned to despise when she was growing up. And now she's helping her own daughters develop a healthy body image and accept themselves—even if their bodies don't happen to meet the standard set by the culture.

If you and I resolutely resist unhealthy attitudes and activities in pursuit of the unattainable and unrealistic, we help free the next generation. We *can* help our daughters, sisters, and friends reorder their thinking about body image, acceptance, and beauty. We can reach out to the next generation and spare them the heartache of trying to meet impossible standards. So much of beauty is self-acceptance. What a wonderful gift—and what an important legacy—to leave behind!

*Never doubt that a small group of thoughtful,
committed citizens can change the world.
Indeed, it is the only thing that ever has.——Margaret Mead*

*Father,*

*thank You for my rich inheritance!*

*Thank You for the unique natural traits that I possess.*

*Forgive me for not recognizing them as treasures*

*that You have given to me alone.*

*Forgive me for the times I've despised*

*my body and put myself down.*

*Help me to cherish those traits I've inherited from my parents,*

*to embrace them with joy,*

*and to honor my family heritage with gratitude.*

*And mostly, Father, help me every day to remember*

*the rich inheritance I have in You.*

*And thank You for the wonderful legacy I will leave behind.*

*Amen*

# CHAPTER TEN

# HOW ARE
# YOU SHAPED?

# A Weight of Glory

He turns my hardship to glory…

*Our light and momentary troubles are achieving for us an eternal glory that far outweighs them all.——2 Corinthians 4:17*

RAISING MY FIVE-POUND dumbbell over my head for the fifteenth time, I clunk the back of my skull. Shaping up can be a real headache!

We think that our shaping comes from the gym, an exercise video, or a daily power walk, but our real shaping—the lasting, eternal, truly significant shaping—comes in a very different way.

Some of my most rigorous shaping recently has taken place nowhere near the gym. For almost eight years before we ever laid eyes on it, Larry and I had a vision for a ranch: a quiet, secluded place where the artistic community could birth screenplays, music, books, fine art, and other creative projects; a private retreat where corporate and government leaders could meet to make important decisions; a restful place of refuge where people in ministry could find healing and restoration; and a peaceful place of solitude for those who just need to hear God's voice again. It was a glorious vision, affirmed by many and confirmed by God.

Now I'm cleaning toilets.

Every step of the way has been hard. I've heard the "glory stories" of many other visions—the miraculous inflow of finances; the miraculous flocking of people to donate time, labor, and money; the miraculous this, the miraculous that. That's not our story.

We're doing this alone, slugging it out bit by painstaking bit. Paying plumbers and electricians, replacing fences and building bridges, buying materials and tools and machinery I'd never even heard of, watching our bank account emptying faster than a leaky water tank. Little by little, year by year, we're finishing the renovations. One guesthouse, then the second, then the lodge. Now we can sleep twenty. I'm reminded that God says if we're faithful in the little, He will give us more. And He has.

He's given me more toilets.

Now I have to be honest: This feels like a real step down. I've spent the last twenty years on a TV soundstage, with makeup artists and hairdressers and costumers meeting my every need. A young man brings morning coffee, and another gently raps at my beautifully appointed motor home to say, "Miss Stafford, we're ready for you on set."

*Ahhhh.... Those were the days,* I reminisce, as I stick my hand in a yellow rubber glove and shove it halfway down a toilet. *Oh, good, only five more to go. And six loads of towels, four loads of sheets, terraces to weed, and tree limbs to haul. Oh, and I can't forget to fill those gopher holes and chase the skunks out of the woodpile.*

I'm thinking of Joseph a lot these days. He was up and he was down. He became the favored son and then was thrown in a pit. He rose to a high position in Potiphar's house, only to be falsely accused and hauled off to jail. He helped others get out of prison and then was forgotten by the men he had helped. Finally, seventeen years after his brothers threw him into the pit, he was elevated to the highest position in the land, just below Pharaoh himself. Sort of puts my measly toilet scrubbing in perspective.

Maybe you've been in a position of visibility, influence, honor, wealth, or power. Maybe, like Joseph, you've been stripped of your position and cast into darkness. And maybe it's happened more than once. You've been released from the dungeon, only to find yourself thrust back there again by hard circumstances. You feel forgotten, abandoned, maybe even hopeless. But the end of Joseph's story holds the key. He understood what God had in mind. "You intended to harm me," he said to his brothers, who had set the whole chain of events in motion, "but God intended it for good to accomplish what is now being done, the saving of many lives" (Genesis 50:20).

Joseph's ups and downs were what God used to shape him into the man who would one day save an entire nation…and from whom would come Jesus of Nazareth, who would one day redeem the entire world.

Our real shaping—the shaping of our hearts—comes through struggle, through hardship, through pain and suffering. Through the flat-out hard stuff of life. It's not produced in comfort or complacency. It happens on the back side of the desert, in a black hole, or in a palace prison. Or maybe through endless toilets. It happens in the lonely and desolate places where we're all alone…except for God.

Our shaping can look a lot like breaking—of our pride, our control, our pasts, our fears…even our dreams. We're stripped of what we've known and what we've relied upon. Even of what we've been promised. Why? Because in our brokenness God can begin to do something through us that we could never even imagine doing on our own.

Like Joseph, we've each been given a dream, a vision. We each have our own land to redeem—our family, our community, our industry, our nation, our generation. And we're being prepared, through all the painful and difficult circumstances in our lives, to take that ground. When we allow God to shape us, we're truly fit—

for life and for loving service to God and to one another. We're being shaped into people of faith, integrity, and purity of heart, people who can be trusted with the dreams that God has placed in us and the purposes He has for us.

And one day, He'll take our five-pound dumbbell—or our toilet brush—and hand us a weight of glory.

*That which is sent by God will only produce the perfection of His glory in your present and future existence.*—*Madame Guyon*

# THE WEIGHT OF THE CROSS

He sympathizes with my weaknesses…

*We have one who has been tempted in every way, just as we are—*
*yet was without sin. Let us then approach the throne of grace*
*with confidence, so that we may receive mercy and find grace*
*to help us in our time of need.*—*Hebrews 4:15–16*

IN *THE INNER LIFE OF SYRIA, Palestine, and the Holy Land,* Isabel Burton wrote: "I saw the desert, it grew upon me. There are times, when I have sorrows, that I hunger and thirst for it."[17] That must have been how Jesus felt when He slipped away from the pressing crowds to hear His Father's voice again. And that must have been how He felt when He stumbled into Gethsemane, desperate for assurance that He was doing His Father's will.

Jesus often went into the desert. If the Son of God had to quiet His heart, steel His soul, and refresh His spirit, how much more do we? His trips into the desert or to the mountainside alone—to pray, fast, listen, or just rest—prepared Him for the final desert experience, His own dark night of the soul—the cross.

I believe that Jesus understood the excruciating agony that awaited Him when the sins of all men of all times would bear down on Him. But even more agonizing, He knew, would be the separation from His Father. For the first time in all of eternity, the godhead would be split, as the sinless Son became sin for us and in His own body carried our guilt and shame so that we would not have to. Spit upon, flogged, and ridiculed, He sacrificed His body through a death designed for criminals, a humiliating torture, an excruciating cruelty. Unspeakable agony, anguish…and loss. I think that the loss of His Father's presence was Jesus' greatest sacrifice. Wrenched from light to utter darkness, the divine became despicable, and His holy name a curse.

That night in Gethsemane, Jesus prayed a prayer that enabled Him to stay the course and take the way of the cross. "My soul is overwhelmed with sorrow to the point of death," He cried, drops of sweat falling like blood to the ground. "Abba, Father.… Take this cup from me. Yet not what I will, but what you will" (Mark 14:34, 36).

It was one night—just one—but it changed everything. It could have gone another way. While Jesus' most trusted friends slept numbly nearby, a heavenly host of warring angels awaited the Father's command to thunder to the rescue of His Son. All of heaven rumbled and churned.

Or…did heaven grow deathly hushed that night?

The long-appointed day, the day anticipated through the millennia, *that* day, had finally come. But suddenly joy mixed with pain. Even all of heaven held its breath when Jesus spoke: "Yet not what I will, but what you will." Reality dawned on a legion of heavenly hosts that victory required a sacrifice: Him. To pay the price, the Father would abandon the Son, and the Son would be separated from the Father.

And utter silence echoed in response to the anguished cries of both.

One man's desert led to our salvation. The Savior walked through the darkest wasteland imaginable, and through His death "fully experienced death in every person's place" (Hebrews 2:9, *The Message*). His dark night of the soul was the dawn of our victory. "Since the children have flesh and blood, he too shared in their humanity so that by his death he might destroy him who holds the power of death—that is, the devil—and free those who all their lives were held in slavery by their fear of death" (Hebrews 2:14–15).

Jesus was like you and me in every way. There is no heartache, pain, isolation, rejection, betrayal, or shame—no desert you can ever walk through—that Jesus did not also endure. The Holy One stepped down from heaven, took our sin onto Himself, and endured the wrath of God so that we would not have to. And now He proudly presents us holy and pure and blameless before His Father.

Jesus has walked through the desert. He understands. How grateful I am that He understands mine.

> *The cross is not a detour or a hurdle*
> *on the way to the kingdom,*
> *nor is it even the way to the kingdom;*
> *it is the kingdom come.—John Howard Yoder*

# REFLECTIONS OF HIS LOVE

---

Feeling defeated, forgotten, overwhelmed, fearful.

"You're being squeezed. I'm letting you fail in your own strength so I can produce something of value."

*What are we supposed to do, Lord?*

"Just believe. Believe Me—believe in Me."

*But Lord, what about all the times You didn't come through—so many deep disappointments?*

"You think of those things as failures. I think of them as fulfilling My purposes. You will serve Me with far more glory after this time."

*Forgive me for my lack of faith; give me grace to believe.*

"How do you think faith gets built? In the fire. Did Moses lead My people without spending forty years on the back side of the desert? Did Joseph rule with authority before spending years in prison and forgotten?"

*I trust You, Lord. I want to have an unshakable faith. Do this work in me I pray. Forgive me, Father. I feel like I take one step forward and three steps back in my growth.*

"I see your growth. I see what's happening in you. Don't be discouraged. I love you...I have not left you."

Jesus, my Savior and Lord,

my heart is overwhelmed,

and my spirit cries out in gratitude for Your amazing sacrifice.

Thank You that You withstood the most painful desert of all,

the desert of the cross, for me.

Thank You for reminding me that there is nothing I go through

that You have not experienced and don't understand.

Thank You that even when I feel alone, I am not.

You walk with me through my painful and desolate times.

Shape me into the woman You have designed me to be,

so that I may fulfill Your purpose and dream for my life.

Amen

# CHAPTER ELEVEN

# BEAUTY REST

# Tender Words in the Wilderness

He speaks tenderly to me...

*"I will allure her, and bring her into the wilderness, and speak tenderly to her."* —*Hosea 2:14, RSV*

SOMETIMES GOD DRAWS us into a quiet or solitary place—or even into the desert of a crisis of faith—so that He can begin to show us the things that need His loving touch. In our daily noise and activities, it's easy to forget how unique, valued, and loved we really are.

Cathy had known God since she was a child and had worked hard all of her life to be "good enough"—nice enough, pretty enough, helpful enough, even righteous enough—to warrant acceptance and approval from people...and from God. She was a leader in the women's ministry of her church, hosted a home fellowship group, and even led a monthly Bible study. Oh, she'd never admit it, of course, but these activities gave Cathy what she needed: constant words of affirmation and approval from others. And though all of these activities were good, they kept her at arm's length from God.

But Cathy began to burn out. She felt tired and resentful, and her feelings were easily hurt. She didn't feel people responding to her in the ways they always had—she no longer felt like the "fair-haired darling." So she took on even more activities to get the recognition she was accustomed to and needed. It didn't work. Soon she began to feel despondent, and then depressed. Finally, she dialed down, closed the door, and surrendered herself to God in the quiet of her easy chair.

*In order to be united to God, you must participate in His infinite stillness.... Your spirit can never arrive in divine union or become one with God until you have been reestablished in His rest and purity.*—Madame Guyon

There the Lord, who had allured her into this desert, began to speak tenderly to her. He came close. He touched her spirit with His and showered her with His love, assuring her of her value and His delight in her. Cathy had never felt the love of God in such a way. She had believed that He accepted her for who she was, but she had never really experienced that acceptance. That day she did. And she began an honest and intimate relationship with God that changed her, radiated out to touch her family, and transformed her ministry.

Cathy learned what Anne Morrow Lindbergh expressed so well:

Certain springs are tapped only when we are alone. The artist knows he must be alone to create; the writer, to work out his thoughts; the musician to compose; the saint, to pray. But women need solitude in order to find again the true essence of themselves.... The problem is not entirely in finding the room of one's own, the time alone, difficult and necessary as this is. The problem is more how to still the soul in the midst of its activities. In fact, the problem is how to feed the soul.[18]

In quiet times of intimacy, God began to show Cathy that it wasn't what she *did* that made Him love her—it was simply who she *was*.

*Listen to God's speech in His wondrous, terrible, gentle, loving, all-embracing silence.*—Catherine de Hueck Doherty

# DESERT REST

*He takes me to a quiet place and gives me rest...*

*"Come with me by yourselves to a quiet place
and get some rest."* —Mark 6:31

DO YOU NEED some rest?

When was the last time you went away anywhere on a private retreat to a secluded place, away from your hectic schedule, daily grind, and incessant noise, just to quiet your anxious thoughts and connect with God again? For just a day, have you secluded yourself from the world to be alone with Him, to let Him speak to your heart and remind you of who He is and who you are? When was the last time you spent just a little while, an hour or even fifteen minutes, when you shut the door—no phone, no noise, no people, no distractions—to sit quietly with Him, rest with Him, and just *be* with Him?

Sounds like a luxury, doesn't it? "My life is too hectic!" you're probably saying. "I'd love to, but who has time for that?"

But it's not a luxury—it's a necessity. Just as we need good food and exercise and plenty of sleep to nourish and refresh our bodies and minds, we need time alone with God to refresh our spirits. Finding a solitary place was a regular practice with Jesus. It should be with us too.

Mark writes that as Jesus' reputation grew, so many people were coming and going that He and the disciples didn't even have a chance to eat. So Jesus said to them, "Come with me by yourselves to a quiet place and get some rest." The Revised Standard Version translates *quiet* place as *lonely* place, and the King James calls it a *desert* place. *The Message* says, "Come off by yourselves; let's take a break and get a little rest."

Isn't that a wonderful invitation? God Himself calls you to come away with Him into the "desert," a quiet place, a solitary place, a place where it's just the two of you. He knows what the demands of life feel like. He knows what it's like to be pulled by people from every side, to be constantly needed. So He invites us, just as He invited His disciples, to slip away from the crowds for a while just to be with Him.

We need time to be alone with our thoughts and feelings. We need time alone to discern, clarify our opinions and ideas, and make decisions…time alone to allow our loving God to help us sort things out, to move and direct us, to minister to our souls. This "desert rest" is more than a quick daily Bible reading and ticking off your prayer requests. This is a settling in, sinking into God's chest, and letting Him speak to you about His love and your life.

*Loneliness is inner emptiness.*
*Solitude is inner fulfillment.—Richard Foster*

Like Jesus, we must sometimes go away from people so that we can be truly present and available when we are with people. "Inward solitude will have outward manifestations," writes Richard Foster.[19]

A listening quiet increases our sensitivity and compassion for others. We become more attuned to their needs and more attentive to their pains. Thomas Merton wrote: "It is in deep solitude that I find the gentleness with which I can truly love my brothers.... Solitude and silence teach me to love my brothers for what they are, not for what they say."[20]

In *The Spirit of the Disciplines,* Dallas Willard writes that "solitude frees us, actually." He says that "the normal course of day-to-day human interactions locks us into patterns of feeling, thought, and action that are geared to a world set against God." In solitude, he says, "we find the psychic distance, the perspective from which we can see, in the light of eternity, the created things that trap, worry, and oppress us."[21]

Are you longing for something more?

Are you craving a fuller experience of God's presence?

Are you yearning to nestle into a place of solitude and rest with Him?

Don't wait for someone to give you permission to rest in Him. Give yourself permission. This "desert rest" is a primary source of strength for the believer. Every few months, or even weeks, arrange for help with the kids and your business, unplug the phone, close the door, and spend the day alone with God. And at least once a year give yourself permission to go on a retreat to a quiet place—the ocean, the mountains, the desert. It is in quiet and solitude with God that we find the peace that is the desire of our heart.

*This is one of the charms of the desert,*
*that removing as it does nearly all the accessories of life,*
*we see the thin thread of necessities on which*
*our human existence is suspended.—Freya Stark*

# DESOLATE BEAUTY

### He knows the way that I take...

*"He knows the way that I take; when he has tested me,
I will come forth as gold."* —Job 23:10

SOMETIMES YOU'RE DRAWN into the desert, but not by choice. Unlike the disciples, you aren't drawn there by the assurance of time alone with the Master; you don't go there at His invitation to rest and refresh.

No, you don't choose this visit to the desert. Circumstances thrust you into a dry and desolate place. The biopsy comes back malignant. You miscarry a long-awaited child, one conceived with the help of medical science and after many years of prayer. You lose a beloved parent. You're wrongly accused of betrayal. You stand help-less as someone you love struggles with a debilitating illness. Deep wounds stretch your marriage so taut that you can't even talk about it. A trusted business partner rips you off, leaving you financially strapped. You're unfairly fired from a job.

All of those things describe my desert. They have all happened in my life. And things like them happen in yours. Health reports, loss, and injustice leave us aching and frightened in the starkness of the desert. Sometimes it may not be a specific event that catapults us into desolation. Maybe there is a crisis within, a crisis of faith or emotions, that leads to our dark night of the soul; a dark night that may last days or weeks, months…even years.

We do not go there willingly. Unlike Jesus, who was led by the Spirit and voluntarily followed God's call into the desert after His baptism, we hunker down on the verdant hillside, heels dug into the earth. We defiantly shake our head at the hand that gently beckons us to come onto the hot, rocky ground. We scan the horizon for the nearest lush hillside we can dash to for comfort.

*He can't be calling me out there. It's too wild and too dangerous, too deserted and too forsaken.*

We don't understand the beauty of this desolate place. We don't grasp the gift and the glory of this dark night of the soul…at least not while we're in it.

*"I thought You loved me!"* we wail. *"Where are You? Why didn't You prevent this?"* Our small minds and selfish hearts are unable to fathom a purpose that goes deeper than our own imaginations.

Sometimes it might be our sin, our rebellion, or our disobedience that produces this desert time. God may be waving smelling salts under our slumbering consciences. Or perhaps we've lost our first love, and our adulterous hearts, drawn away from our Beloved, have ended up in this dry and desolate place, where God invites us to come back home. Or perhaps we can see no reason at all, save God's sovereignty.

Whatever the reason, our obvious sin or God's sovereign mystery, we feel naked, and we remember the word from the prophet Hosea to the adulterous Israel, "Otherwise I will strip her naked and make her as bare as on the day she was born; I will make her like a desert, turn her into a parched land, and slay her with thirst" (Hosea 2:3).

So we are stripped bare of everything we have that makes us who we are and gives us what we think we need. Nothing works anymore: no natural ability, no good fortune, no amount of favor, no amount of self-sufficiency. We can't "fix" anything. Nothing changes our circumstances. All is beyond our control. And all feels out of control.

We hate it. We feel we're being punished. Our hearts simultaneously rise in indignation and faint in weakness. Grief and loss are so excruciating that we think they will surely kill us.

*I've served You all these years. What have I done wrong? Are You punishing me?*

We feel like Job searching for God. "But if I go to the east, he is not there; if I go to the west, I do not find him. When he is at work in the north, I do not see him; when he turns to the south, I catch no glimpse of him" (Job 23:8–9).

*God, I don't see You. Where are You?*

But He sees us. In the very next verse, Job says, "But he knows the way that I take; *when he has tested* me, I will come forth as gold (Job 23:10, emphasis added). God knows the way that we take. He knows better than we do. And He will test us. Jesus Himself was tested and tried during forty days in the desert before He was released into the ministry for which He was born. Can we expect less? Like Job, we can only pray that when we are tested—not if, but *when*—we will come forth as gold.

Oswald Chambers says:

> Our faith has to be worked out in actualities. We shall be
> scattered…into inner desolations and made to know what
> internal death to God's blessings means. Are we prepared
> for this? It is not that we choose it, but that God engineers
> our circumstances so that we are brought there. Until we
> have been through that experience, our faith is bolstered
> up by feelings and by blessings. When once we get there,
> no matter where God places us or what the inner desola-

tions are, we can praise God that all is well…. Darkness comes by the sovereignty of God. Are we prepared to let God do as He likes with us—prepared to be separated from conscious blessings?[22]

Have you been led into this desert? Have you felt stripped bare, tested through hard circumstances and painful desert silence? God knows the way that you take. He is with you, even in the painful testing. Remain faithful to your Beloved in the midst of the heartache, and when He has tested you, you will come forth as gold.

*I am amazed at the power that comes to us through suffering;*
*we are worth nothing without the cross.*
*Of course, I tremble and agonize while it lasts and all my*
*words about the beneficial effects of suffering vanish under torture.*
*But when it is all over, I look back on the experience*
*with deep appreciation, and am ashamed that*
*I bore it with so much bitterness.* —*Fenelon*

# Springs in the Desert

He makes my wilderness like Eden…

*"I will make rivers flow on barren heights, and springs within the valleys. I will turn the desert into pools of water, and the parched ground into springs."* —*Isaiah 41:18*

WE THINK THAT the desert is to be avoided, a place where only the worst are brought: the criminals, the wicked, the outcasts. Or maybe it's only for the best, the place where the great saints of old were brought: John the Baptizer, the desert fathers, St. John of the Cross, or St. Teresa of Avila. Maybe Madame Guyon or Thomas Merton. But not me. I'm neither too wicked nor too righteous for the desert.

Your Job friends agree. Drawn like sharks to blood, they chime, "Where's your faith?" or "What hidden sin have you not confessed?" or "What generational curse has befallen you?" or "Just rebuke this attack from the devil and claim your victory!" Maybe some of what they say is right.

But maybe not.

A. W. Tozer once said that it is doubtful that God can bless a man greatly until He has hurt him deeply. God's goodness doesn't always come wrapped in the expected. Just look at the manger…and the cross. Maybe your gentle Lover is wooing you through this dark and arid and impossible time, drawing you into a deeper place in His heart for a second betrothal:

Therefore I am now going to allure her; I will lead her into the desert and speak tenderly to her. There I will give her back her vineyards, and will make the Valley of Achor a door of hope. There she will sing as in the days of her youth, as in the day she came up out of Egypt.

HOSEA 2:14–15

Even as God draws us into the desert of our lives, He does so to speak tenderly to us, to reassure, comfort, encourage. He shows His love in the midst of judgment…or what feels like it.

On the west side of the Dead Sea, between Qumran and Masada, lies En Gedi, an oasis of green bursting out of the brown desert…and one of my favorite places on earth. There, three thousand years ago, David hid from Saul in the caves and cliffs, finding refuge and refreshment in the welcome streams, waterfalls, and tropical greenery of the Judean wilderness. Like the oasis of En Gedi springing up in the Judean wilderness, a door of hope opens onto our Achor, our own valley of trouble.

Just as David found refuge and refreshment at those springs in the desert, the Lord will bring springs to your parched heart in your desert. It may not be the refreshment you desire—the child or the marriage, the healing, the job or the finances—but it will be a living water that quenches with a sweetness that satisfies what you've really been longing for: an intimacy with Him that words cannot express.

"I will betroth you to me forever," He says; "I will betroth you to me in righteousness and in justice, in steadfast love, and in mercy. I will betroth you to me in faithfulness; and you shall know the LORD" (Hosea 2:19–20, RSV). The Hebrew word for *know* is *yada*, a word that also refers to intimate marital relations. With abandon, you drink deep at the oasis of His springs. As His living water washes over you, nourishing and quenching you completely, you realize: He is good.... He is sovereign.... He is worthy of your trust.... He is enough.

You think you've been abandoned in this dry, desolate place. You feel you're walking alone over cracked, parched earth. Its hardened crust mirrors the landscape of your heart. The air never moves. Stillness. Nothing as far as you can see except sameness and emptiness. Then you feel the hot desert wind on your neck, and suddenly you realize that it's His breath, His nearness, His voice. He is whispering tenderly to you. He is comforting you in your ruins and making your wastelands like the garden of the Lord. He is near.

The beauty of our desolation is His nearness. He strips away the distractions. He peels away our veneer. And in that barren place, He exposes our idols. In His love, He gently pries open our fingers, and as we yield our idols of wood and gold to our merciful Lover, He gives us Himself. It's in these intimate times, even when—or perhaps especially when—we are in the desert, that God calls out our true beauty. And we fall down onto boiling sand in worship and adoration of our King.

Is there anything more beautiful than the starkness of the desert?

*Beauty is mysterious as well as terrible.*
*God and devil are fighting there,*
*and the battlefield is the heart of man.*—*Dostoyevsky*

# REFLECTIONS OF HIS LOVE

He comes in like a flood.

"Let not your heart be troubled. Let Me free your heart, free you from the cage it's been locked up in. My understanding of good and evil is so different from yours. What may appear evil is often My best. I draw you into the desert and there speak lovingly to you. I will answer your prayer for discernment about what is good and what is evil. And in those days you will be an encouragement to My people. You will strengthen weak knees, My light will shine from you, because you have been there."

O Father,

wash over me now.

I am overwhelmed by Your compassion and love,

by the ways You draw me back to intimacy with You.

Come as You promise, and make the barren wilderness of my sin,

my heartaches, disappointments, and suffering,

blossom into the beauty of the Garden of Eden.

Let Your kingdom come and Your will be done

through all the hard circumstances of my life.

Help me to find that place of rest with

You that my heart hungers for.

Drive away the fears and distractions and excuses.

Help me to say yes to You.

Because You are with me, let joy and gladness be found there,

thanksgiving and the voice of song.

Amen

# CHAPTER TWELVE

# UNIQUELY YOU

# BUSTED!

### He gives me everything I need...

*His divine power has given us everything*
*we need for life and godliness.—2 Peter 1:3*

ON *MATLOCK* I played Andy Griffith's law partner, Michelle, so I wore a suit nearly every day for the five years I did the show. But in one episode my character got to wear an evening gown, and the costume designer and I were ecstatic! Jean-Pierre Dorleac designed a gorgeous gown for me—sky blue satin jersey that hugged every inch of my body. Spaghetti straps crisscrossed to a plunging back and a fishtail train. It was cut on the bias and moved like liquid with every step I took. If I do say so myself, Jean-Pierre made me look like a million bucks!

We finished the last fitting and stood in front of the mirror admiring his handiwork. It was gorgeous. But there was just one thing missing. I needed a little...oh, I dunno...*something more.* I needed a little extra *oomph.* I needed bust pads. You know, to give me that "little something extra." It would make all the difference. Then I'd look fabulous. Yup, bust pads would do it.

"I gotta have bust pads," I told Jean-Pierre.

"No, no, *no,*" he said. "You look fine just the way it is. You don't need them."

I dug in my four-inch heels. "But it's my *one* chance on the show to dress like this! I'll never get to do it again. I *need* those bust pads! I really, *really* need them—please, please, please!"

I persisted unmercifully until he finally relented. Like a petulant child, he handed over the bust pads.

Smile. Sigh. Now I'm lookin' good!

After two full hours of painting, I emerged from the makeup trailer with sweeping lashes, shimmering eye shadow, rosy red glossed lips, and big hair.

I'm lookin' gooood!

I opened the stage door. A shaft of sunlight framed me like a spotlight, and every head snapped toward me. As I walked onto the set, people stopped dead in their tracks. You could've heard a pin drop.

Yup, I'm lookin' *real* gooood!

I sashayed across the stage. Dead silence. The only sound was the clip-clip-clip of my silver stiletto heels on the concrete floor. Jaws dropped. Eyes bulged. Finally, still gaping, the crew began to whisper among themselves.

Now I *know* I'm lookin' good.

Then I overheard one of the guys say, "Wow, look at Nancy. I always thought she was kinda pretty. I never noticed that lump in her midriff before." I glanced down, ever so unobtrusively. An errant bust pad had slipped and lodged halfway to my belly button.

Busted!

I roared in laughter, reached in, yanked it out, pulled the other one out, and tossed them across the set. "Okay, okay! Let's just do television!"

I was ribbed about that for years.

Like my mother always used to say, "Honey it's what's on the inside that counts." The moral of that tale: You might *act* like you have it all together, and you might *think* you look good on the out-side, but believe me, what's on the inside *will* eventually show through! So be real, be genuine, just be yourself. The truth of the matter is that God has given us everything we need for life and god-liness. The rest is just…stuffing!

*Why not be one's self?*
*That is the whole secret of a successful appearance.*
*If one is a greyhound,*
*why try to look like a Pekingese?*—*Edith Sitwell*

# THE PERFECT PART

He knows me...

*"Before I formed you in the womb I knew you,*
*before you were born I set you apart."* —*Jeremiah 1:5*

I WAS THIRTY-FIVE when I got married. I'd waited a loooong time to find a godly man with whom to share my life—one who understood, accepted, and appreciated me for who I am. After I met Larry, we dated for a year and a half, getting to know what each other's lives were like and the demands they made on us. We diligently prayed. We sought wise counsel. And then we were engaged for a year. Let's just say we didn't rush into marriage.

My husband and I make an unusual pair. There aren't a lot of pastors I know who are married to actresses. If you believe what Jean Kerr wrote, movie actors are just ordinary, mixed-up people—with agents. So though I'm not exactly "normal," Larry tells me that I'm not your typical actress. And he's not your typical pastor, either. He's also an artist—a musician who has ministered to the creative community in L.A. for over twenty-five years. We're on the same wavelength. It's a perfect fit!

The wonderful church we were involved in at the time was incredibly supportive. No one ever made me feel "funny" because I was an actress. They supported us, they loved me, and they loved what I did for a living. So I was surprised, to say the least, at something that happened at my wedding reception.

A perfect balmy breeze wafted through the lush garden perched on the bluffs of the Pacific Ocean. A string quartet played classical music, and servers offered salmon, roast beef, and fancy pastas at elegant food stations. Dear friends hugged my neck and dabbed their eyes in joy as I strolled from table to table.

Then, while I was chatting with pals from the film industry, a friend—a musician and painter as well as a pastor—elbowed his way through the crowd. I knew that he loved us and was thrilled for us. He gave me a bear hug. Then, with a big smile but in total sincerity, he asked, "Nancy, now that you're a pastor's wife, when are you going to get out of that wicked business?"

I almost dropped my bouquet of baby roses in his plate of eggplant ziti. I blinked a few times. *He's pulling my leg, right? What a teaser! We're here at my wedding reception, surrounded by my Matlock "family" and he's making a joke—right? No?*

No.

I laughed politely with him, still not quite sure whether he was kidding or not. I don't remember the next half-hour of my reception.

Who I am and what I do are what make me unique. They are what qualify me to play the part God has assigned me. And *your* uniqueness is what enables you to fulfill your special role.

Embrace your uniqueness. It's the very thing that God gave you to distinguish you. It's the very thing that's needed. No one else can do what you've been specifically created to do. The only time your uniqueness needs to yield is when it conflicts with the character of Christ. Otherwise, play the part God has written for you. You are perfectly cast!

*It's the worst of all sins to sacrifice your uniqueness.*
*Because it suggests that God hasn't done*
*a good job.——Jamie Buckingham*

# No Comparison

## I am wonderfully made...

*I praise you because I am fearfully and wonderfully made;
your works are wonderful, I know that full well.*—Psalm 139:14

WHEN ELIZABETH'S DAUGHTER was six, she insisted on dressing herself for school every day. My friend was appalled when her little daughter regularly scampered into her classroom in mismatched socks, chartreuse printed pants, her older brother's high-top tennis shoes...and her pink ballet tutu. *What will people think? Look how pretty the other little girls look! Why can't she let me dress her like that?*

Another pal of mine would love to wear trendier clothes that better express her fresh, young attitude, but her more conservative friends ridiculed her when she tried. Yet another friend was happy to have coffee with friends in their homes but was too embarrassed to invite them to hers because it wasn't as "nice" as theirs.

Why do we compare ourselves to others so much?

The beauty of Christ's grace is that we no longer have to look to others to assess our worth or position. We look to the Cross. We gaze into His face. We take Him at His word.

Jesus wants to set us free from the pressure of comparing ourselves to others and trying to keep up appearances—to look or act perfect, have the perfect home, drive the right car, belong to the right circles, send our kids to the right schools. Even in the church, we can become so religious—so bound to be what's expected of us in order to look right—that we can lose our individuality, the very thing God gave us to set us apart.

*All men are born originals. Most die copies—*
*usually because the church made them that way.*—Myles Munroe

Here's a secret: Your beauty lies in your uniqueness.

World-famous choreographer Agnes de Mille once told fellow dancer Martha Graham:

> There is a vitality, a life-force, an energy, a quickening that is translated through you into action and because there is only one of you in all of time, this expression is unique. And if you block it, it will never exist through any other medium and [it will] be lost. The world will not have it. It is not your business to determine how good it is nor how valuable nor how it compares with other expressions. It is your business to keep it yours clearly and directly, to keep the channel open.[23]

As followers of Christ, we, most of all, are free to celebrate and express God's unique creation in ourselves and others.

God made each of us different for a different purpose. There has never been anyone quite like *you*...and there never will be again! Realizing that and accepting your uniqueness affects how you see yourself, how you connect with those around you, and even how you serve God and glorify Him with your life. You begin to embrace— not just tolerate—your face, your hair, your figure. You begin to enjoy and even play up your special attributes, even your quirks, as the remarkable gifts from God that distinguish you.

Diana Vreeland, the great lady of fashion and editor of *Vogue,* once had an assistant who had a very long nose. He grew a beard thinking that a bigger chin would change the proportion of his face and make his nose appear smaller as a result.

"You're wrong!" Vreeland told him. "If it's big, make it bigger. Assume it!"

What a wonderful definition of style! Let's assume it for ourselves! Let's start to see perfection as ordinary and imperfection as unique, singular, original. See it as the definition of *you.* And then look for ways to express your uniqueness in what you wear, how you look, how you behave. Let's broaden the definitions of beauty and style instead of being enslaved to others people's standards.

Maybe it's your offbeat sense of humor, your ability to find the amusing in the mundane. Perhaps it has something to do with how you always encourage others or the way you gently touch someone's arm when you're listening to her. It could be the way you breeze into the room—that expectancy and bounce in your step. Maybe it's the breadth of your dreams. Or the depth of your passion. Or it could be the sparkle in your eyes or your contagious laughter. I'm talking about a beauty that defies size and shape—one that has absolutely nothing to do with body type, color, and age.

And as Christians, we have an opportunity to show the world how an intimate and vibrant relationship with Jesus Christ transforms us from the inside out. As He moves us from glory to glory, His grace changes everything about us—our minds, our hearts, and how we feel about ourselves, because, frankly, the focus begins to shift from us to Him. We begin to glow with an inner radiance and confidence—the hallmarks of real beauty.

Your uniqueness is God's great gift to you. Don't sacrifice it. Don't despise it. It really is where your beauty lies. It's your greatest beauty secret.

*Always be a first-rate version of yourself,*
*instead of a second-rate version of somebody else.—Judy Garland*

# REFLECTIONS OF HIS LOVE

Meditating today on 1 Kings 7:14: The bronze craftsman, Huram, came to King Solomon, and "did all the work assigned to him."

*Lord, I want to be a Huram, one who does all the work given to him—the creative, inspired work that You allow me to do, that You even created me to do.*

"What keeps you from it? What are you so afraid of?"

*That I won't live up to Your expectations.*

"Are you afraid of not living up to *My* expectations, or yours? You don't have to be anyone else—no more comparisons. Huram was highly skilled in all kinds of bronze work. He did the bronze work. Not the wood work, not the silver work, not the gold work. He did what he was created to do. He did it excellently.

"He didn't do the whole thing. He worked alongside others who were excellent in their giftings, each bringing a portion, none more beautiful or important than the other. Together they created the beauty that allowed My people to see My splendor, to worship Me.

"I inhabited what they created, and the entire population was blessed. Each craftsman's contribution was beautiful, but all took a backseat to the One whose train fills the Temple."

# MIRROR, MIRROR ON THE WALL

I am accepted in the Beloved…

*Accept one another, then, just as Christ accepted you,
in order to bring praise to God.*——Romans 15:7

ONCE UPON A TIME in a kingdom far, far away lived Snow White. She was happy and contented growing up in her castle, even though her stepmother, the Queen, was exceedingly vain. Every day, the Queen asked her magic mirror the same question: "Mirror, mirror on the wall, who's the fairest of them all?" As long as the mirror said that the Queen was the fairest in the land, all was well. Years passed, and Snow White grew into a beautiful woman. And then one day it happened: The Queen's mirror told her that Snow White was the fairest in the land. In a jealous rage, the Queen gave her stepdaughter a poisoned apple.

It happens in real life as well as in fairy tales. It's called making comparisons, and it can be deadly.

Angela never felt that her mirror was magic; it never told her what she wanted to hear. "All my life, I've felt unattractive. I look around at college and see all these other girls—they're gorgeous. They have long, pretty hair. Mine is thin and ugly. I've cut it, permed it, even colored it, and it's still not right. They're comfortable talking to people, but then they have great bodies. I have no chest, huge hips, ugly skin, and I hate my nose." She laughs. "There's nothing I really like about myself. If I looked different, I'm sure I'd be happy."

Angela and the wicked Queen actually have a lot in common. They define their worth and significance by what they look like...in comparison to others. How about you? As daughters of the King, we know better. We know that our worth isn't measured by how we look to others, or even how we look to ourselves, but only in how we look to God...and only in comparison with who He created us to be.

When you compare yourself with others, you just find yourself competing with them. It's tragic to think how many people actually spend their whole lives competing with someone else. And it's not always about appearance. We can compare and compete with each other's talents, achievements, social status, family life, money, favor...even spiritual gifts. Most people probably don't even realize how competitive they are.

Some may constantly compare themselves with their daughters, sisters, mothers, girlfriends, and acquaintances. And if they perceive others as more attractive, more accomplished, more...anything...they feel that they themselves just don't measure up.

Their assessment that others are "more" just makes them feel "less." They feel inferior, inadequate, insecure. "If I'm not the best, if I'm not the fairest, then I must be nothing." And they can react in a couple of ways.

Some, like Angela, their insecurity making them tentative and self-conscious, may become shy and withdrawn and slink into the background for fear of ridicule. They condemn themselves, maybe even begin to loathe themselves, because they're sure they can't measure up to the standards they think others around them have met.

Unfortunately, there are also women whose insecurities and envy provoke a different response, one more like the wicked Queen's.

When they view others as more attractive than themselves, they react with hostility. They can be cold, sarcastic, downright rude. If their magic mirror says they're the fairest, they're fine. If it doesn't, don't eat the apples. Too much competition for too few princes can make them jealous, resentful, angry, and sometimes even violent.

Ever had someone say a mean, nasty remark for no apparent reason or put you down with a sarcastic comment couched in humor? You just had an encounter with the spirit of Snow White's stepmom. The person wasn't wicked, but her reaction was. Putting you down made her feel like the fairest again...if only for the briefest moment.

Come on now, let's be honest. Truth be told, there's a little wicked Queen in all of us. We all struggle with the broken part of us that wants and needs to be the fairest in the land. And as long as we determine our worth on the basis of comparisons—or some earthly prince's unwavering adoration—our competitiveness and jealousies will rule us.

Ugh! Why do we react like that? Rather than celebrating the achievements or appearance of others, we want to squash them (gossip, anyone?), because it's only when we scramble to balance precariously at the top of the heap that we think we are noticed. So we jab and cut, manipulate and murder, at least in the dark little recesses of our minds. We offer a poisoned apple through our poisoned thoughts. And yet we never do feel confident of the prince's affection or the kingdom's undying adoration.

Because tomorrow we meet Sleeping Beauty; and the next day, Cinderella.

Comparisons just leave us feeling worse about ourselves and rob us of the joy of appreciating the beauty in others. The self-focus becomes pervasive, pathological, overpowering. And as happened to the Queen, in the end it can be our downfall.

Do you compare yourself with others? Do you judge yourself by comparing your face or body, your life or achievements with someone else's? How do you measure your value and significance? Like the Queen in the fairy tale, the mirror you're looking in is distorting your view. What's reflected in that mirror has nothing to do with who you really are.

The question "Who am I?" isn't answered by gazing at yourself. The answer comes when you shift your focus to God, who defines, redeems, and reconciles you through the person of Jesus Christ. He shows you that He adores you, that He thinks you're fabulous just as you are, *and* that He has other daughters that are every bit as special to Him as you are and that He loves just as much. You don't have to be what everyone else considers the "fairest" to be secure in the Prince's love and acceptance; you already are.

So put down that magic mirror. It's distorting your view. Look in God's mirror—the mirror of God's Word—to tell you who you are. When we're established in that truth, we're no longer jealous of each other's success, beauty, or attention. Instead, we're able to wholeheartedly encourage and bring out the beauty in one another.

*Never compete. Never. Watching the other guy is what kills all forms of energy.*—Diana Vreeland

Lord,

thank You that before I was formed in the womb,

You had me in mind and created me just as I am.

You gave me a unique personality and distinctive physical traits.

Help me to delight in my uniqueness

and to realize the wonderful truth

that I am unlike anyone else You have ever made!

I've been created to give You glory, Lord, in ways that only I can.

Help me to glorify You through my life—

and my body—every day.

Help me always to look in Your mirror, Lord.

Forgive me for the times I compare myself to others.

Enlarge my heart. Keep me from envy and jealousy.

Help me be a woman who encourages

and delights in the beauty of others.

Amen

# CHAPTER THIRTEEN

# THE KINGDOM COLLECTION

# CLOTHED WITH LOVE

He clothes me with Himself...

*For all of you who were baptized into Christ
have clothed yourselves with Christ.—Galatians 3:27*

IT ALL STARTED with a dress....

Gossamer gray organza layered over pink. A little round Peter Pan collar. Poofy crinolines and ruffled panties. Patent leather Mary Janes and lacy socks. I was a vision for my two-year-old portrait.

I leaned against the shaggy, carpet-covered box at Olan Mills Studios, trying my best to imitate the man behind the camera who showed me how to place my little chin in my little hand, cupped just so. I hesitated, maybe because even at age two I realized that it was a phony pose, and that got his ire. His face turned red, his eyebrows knit, and he bellowed something...loudly. Forever after, my two-year-old portrait reveals my fear-struck face, quivering lip, and brimming eyes. (Hmm...no wonder my brother's baby pictures are the only ones framed in the hallway.) Mom was so mad at that mean old man that she let me play in my brand-new gray organza dress all day long. That's where it started.

It was all Mom's fault. An incredible seamstress, she made beautiful clothes for me before I could even walk. But the gray organza number was always my favorite. My second favorite was the one she made for me in first grade. It was a navy blue jumper held together by big red buttons at the shoulders, with a smokestack train and butterflies embroidered all around. A perfect circle, it stood straight out when I spun around. "I'm the only girl in first grade with a maternity dress!" I breathlessly exclaimed to Mom.

More great outfits followed: the sixth-grade Easter dress that looked like an English garden, the wild paisley bell-bottoms and midriff shirt in high school, and the traffic-stopping evening suit for the Key Club dance, made of upholstery fabric that looked suspiciously like our dining room chairs. "Just don't sit down for dinner," my brother remarked dryly. "We'll never find you." I didn't care—my suit was spectacular.

My grandmother's vintage linens were transformed into a camisole top. Our family's gold Christmas tree skirt became a one-shouldered minidress costume for the Star Trek theme of the Miss Fort Lauderdale Pageant. And a bed sheet, bought on sale for three dollars, was turned into a skirt and cowl-neck halter that had people stopping me on the street to ask where I bought it.

With every outfit Mom made me, she clothed me with her love. With every piece she created, she gave me a piece of herself. When I wore her clothes, I felt her care, her attention, and her love. Clothes lovingly created by someone dear to you are treasures, and remembering the ones Mom made for me always reminds me of my greatest treasure…and my favorite garment.

I'll never forget the day I got it. I've worn it every day since 1986, but it's still my most cherished garment. It isn't flashy, but it's timeless, and I'll wear it forever. It's white as snow, bright as light, and perfect. I received it as a gift. Although it cost me nothing, it cost Jesus everything. He made it out of pure love. And when Jesus slipped it on me, I felt His arms enfold me and His eyes adore me. And I was changed forever.

# A New Season

He dresses me in rich garments…

*The angel said… "Take off his filthy clothes." Then he said to Joshua, "See, I have taken away your sin, and I will put rich garments on you."* —Zechariah 3:4

It's a new season. The fashion designers are showing off their new creations.

Pattern makers cut and recut, drapers pin and align, seamstresses work round the clock, and beaders add hand-sewn embellishments. Fashion designers scurry about, adding their signature finishing touches. Then, amid flashbulbs popping and celebrities shopping, the latest collections are unveiled on the catwalks in Paris, Milan, and New York.

It seemed like only yesterday that last season's designs made their debut down the runway. But, fickle as fashion is, they're already being cast onto the ho-hum pile of been-there, done-that rags, making way for the new shining stars on the runway. It's out with the old, in with the new, as designers move ahead, refining their new creations…and never looking back. What worked last year just isn't acceptable now. Every year they create something new, more artistic, more creative, more exciting…and more beautiful.

Sitting in the audience at the New York collections, I realized that that's how the Master Designer dresses us. We are His creation.

When we come to Him, it's out with the old, in with the new. What may have worked for us before doesn't cut it anymore. What was once acceptable to us isn't worthy of us now.

Paul explained it to the Colossians this way:

> You used to walk in these ways, in the life you once lived.
> But now you must rid yourselves of all such things as these:
> anger, rage, malice, slander, and filthy language from your
> lips. Do not lie to each other, since you have taken off your
> old self with its practices and have put on the new self, which
> is being renewed in knowledge in the image of its Creator.
> COLOSSIANS 3:7–10

Each season of our life, as we allow Him to, God removes the last vestiges of our old, outdated garments. Like the angel did for Joshua, He takes off our filthy rags and puts a rich garment on us. He takes our sin and dresses us in His new collection—His Kingdom Collection.

He clothes us in garments of salvation and wraps us in robes of His own righteousness. Paul tells us what our new design looks like:

> Therefore, as God's chosen people, holy and dearly loved,
> clothe yourselves with compassion, kindness, humility,
> gentleness and patience. Bear with each other and forgive
> whatever grievances you may have against one another.
> Forgive as the Lord forgave you. And over all these virtues
> put on love, which binds them all together in perfect
> unity. Let the peace of Christ rule in your hearts.… And
> be thankful.… And whatever you do, whether in word or
> deed, do it all in the name of the Lord Jesus, giving thanks
> to God the Father through him.
> COLOSSIANS 3:12–15, 17

Being the perfect designer that He is:

God is putting the finishing touches on the salvation work
he began when we first believed. We can't afford to waste a
minute, must not squander these precious daylight hours
in frivolity and indulgence, in sleeping around and dissipa-
tion, in bickering and grabbing everything in sight. Get
out of bed and get dressed! Don't loiter and linger, waiting
until the very last minute. Dress yourselves in Christ, and
be up and about!
ROMANS 13:13–14, THE MESSAGE

It's a new season. The Master Designer is putting His finishing
touches on you. He's already wrapped you in His glory and His
splendor. Now will you give up last season's clothes? Will you let
Him take away your old rags, your outmoded garments…your old
habits and reactions, your old fears and insecurities, your past and
your pain and your disappointments? He's designed something new
for you—something more creative, more fulfilling, more flattering,
more exciting…and more beautiful.

It's a one-of-a-kind Designer original. It fits perfectly. It feels
comfortable. It will never go out of style. It's a new season, and the
Master Designer is showing off His new creation—you! Now hit the
catwalk of your life…and strut your stuff!

*It's not the dress that makes the woman,
but the woman that makes the dress.—Coco Chanel*

# THE DANCE

He wraps me in a robe of righteousness...

*I delight greatly in the Lord; my soul rejoices in my God.
For he has clothed me with garments of salvation
and arrayed me in a robe of righteousness.—Isaiah 61:10*

GOD HAS DONE such a work of healing and restoration in my life. He has brought me to a place of deep peace and rest and confidence in Him, largely because of something He showed me a few years ago.

I was still struggling with not feeling very confident and secure in who I was. How I felt about myself still depended too much on my circumstances. I felt accepted and valued when I was being validated by Hollywood, but when I wasn't, I didn't. And at the time, I wasn't. I wasn't working as much as I wanted to be, so I was wrestling with insecurities: *I must not be thin enough, pretty enough, young enough, talented enough.* I was still responding out of old wounds and past rejections, and I was hearing those old tapes in my head: *Who do you think you are? You're ugly. You're clumsy. We don't want you.* I was still letting the lies of my past tell me who I was.

Can you relate to any of this? Does this ever sound like you? Even when we know the truth in our spirits, our hearts and souls and minds don't always remember. That's why we have to be regenerated, renewed...and reminded.

I knew that there were areas deep in my heart where I hadn't let

God in—places I didn't really trust Him with and, frankly, places I didn't really think He wanted to be. I knew how unlovely and unlovable I was. Why would a holy and perfect God want to be there? I guess my secret fear was that my deepest suspicions would be confirmed and He would reject me too.

*Lord, please bring an end to this once and for all,* I prayed. *Help me to know who I am in You. I don't want to struggle with these insecurities anymore!* As I was praying, the Lord gave me a beautiful picture, and its truth has brought healing to the deep places within me.

I was standing in a huge grand ballroom. Jesus was standing across the room from me, holding out a gorgeous robe. It looked like a robe that royalty would wear. It was luminous and shining, just like His face. It was absolutely beautiful. Then Jesus walked over to me and very tenderly and very proudly wrapped me up in my new robe…His robe. He held me for a long time and then took my hand…and we danced. It was tender and intimate and totally freeing. And when it was over, the Lord put a passage from Psalm 18 in my mind:

I looked it up, and this is what it says:

He reached down from on high and took hold of me;
> he drew me out of deep waters.
He rescued me from my powerful enemy.
> He brought me out into a spacious place;
he rescued me because he delighted in me.

PSALM 18:16–17, 19

At that moment something broke in me. My heart and mind and soul caught up with my spirit, and I finally *got* it: God wanted me and He rescued me. He knows me and He delights in me.

If your mind is telling you lies like *you're not worth much, you're stupid, nobody wants you,* I want to tell you how God sees you—because He sees you very differently than you see yourself. Once you've accepted Jesus' gift of forgiveness of sin, when God looks at you, He sees the perfection of Jesus. He sees you clothed in the righteousness and wrapped in the splendor and majesty of His only Son. In His eyes you are pure and blameless, His elect, His chosen, His own daughter.

You are no longer the person that grew up believing the lies that now identify you. He's taken all that away. You are a new creation in Christ. You have a new identity. You're not who you were. You are "Christ in You"…and God delights in you!

What God wants more than anything else is a close relationship and deep intimacy with you. Don't be afraid. Let Him lead you out of the bondage of lies into a spacious place of freedom. Take His hand, join Him on the dance floor, look full into His face, and let Him show you who you *really* are, just as He did for me.

# REFLECTIONS OF HIS LOVE

My dear friend Judie Lawson wrote the lyrics to this song.
It touches me deeply every time I hear it.

## WEDDING FEAST OF THE LAMB

There is a place prepared for me
A table by the crystal sea
where my Beloved bids me rest
and gently lean upon His breast
He dries my tears, He breaks my chains
He binds my wounds, He heals my pain
He soothes my tired and troubled soul
He fills my cup, it overflows
The finest wine, the choicest bread
By His own nail scarred hands I am fed
He hides my shame in holy dress
He clothes me with His righteousness
He lifts my veil, He draws me close
proclaims me His to the heavenly host
While angels sing His reverence
He leads me in a sacred dance
There is a place by the crystal sea
where my Beloved waits for me.
He bids me come just as I am
To the wedding feast of the Lamb.

Lyrics by Judie Lawson.
© 1995, Pyewacket Frog / (ASCAP). Used by permission.

# A DESIGNER LABEL

I bear His name…

*You are among us, O Lord,
and we bear your name.* —*Jeremiah 14:9*

AT A CHARITY DINNER I sat next to a woman in a lovely slate blue suit. It complemented her ivory skin and made her eyes pop. "What a beautiful suit on you!" I said when we were introduced. "Gucci," she shot back in a tone I interpreted to mean *I wouldn't wear anything less.* Her eyes quickly ran me up and down. "Whose is that?" she asked. The *that* was a little too drawn out for my taste, and I detected a smidgen of disdain as her X-ray eyes bored into me. I was sure she could read my label right through my Adam's apple.

Shame on me. My rebellion kicked in, mixed with a healthy dose of mischief. "It's mine," I said offhandedly. "Oh, you mean who's the *designer?* Hmm…can't really remember. I've had it for*ever.* Got it on sale. Eighty-nine dollars, I think." She blinked a couple of times as if to say, *Who is this person?* I smiled. She softened and warmed. Her defenses came down. By dessert she was telling me about her marriage problems.

Funny how some people throw around the names of designers as if they were personal pals, exchanging label names like some folks exchange "howdy-do's." I do have some friends who will wear *only* top name designers. From jeans and T-shirts to suits, shoes, and handbags, every item has to have the right logo: Chanel's interlocking *C,* Ralph Lauren's crest or polo-playing horseman, or Nike's swoosh. Other labels don't get the same kind of instant recognition but are nonetheless easy to identify by their style: Armani's classic silhouette, Banana Republic's clean simplicity, Manolo Blahnik's perfect shoe, and Gap's indigo jeans.

We can usually tell something about people from the designer labels they choose to wear. Your designer label announces something about you to the world. You're classic and sophisticated. Or edgy and trendsetting. Maybe soft and romantic, or athletic and sporty. Some might choose a particular label because it means quality and craftsmanship; others because it creates an image or confers status. Your label tells the world what you value and how you want to be perceived.

> *Who said that clothes make a statement?*
> *What an understatement that was.*
> *Clothes never shut up.*—*Susan Brownmiller*

Now, I love fine fashion as much as the next guy—or gal. I appreciate it, and I enjoy the opportunities I have to wear it. But sometimes we can spend a tremendous amount of time and energy making sure we are wearing the right "name." And if we don't have a clear identity and confidence in who we really are, we can tend to rely on our clothes to give us a name—a sense of self-worth and a feeling of importance. We look for a fancy label to give *us* a label, an image, an identity.

Sometimes we wear other kinds of labels, ones that don't have designer names but which are designed, all right—by the enemy of our souls—to hurt us and keep us from living in the truth and walking in the fullness of our true identity. These are labels that others may have given us over the years, or even ones we've given ourselves. Often we've worn them for so long that we've gotten comfortable wearing them. They have names like *stupid, lazy, loser, ugly, victim, worthless....* The list goes on and on.

Or maybe the label we wear has to do with our heritage or ethnicity. Maybe a bit of pride creeps in because of our prestigious family name, wealth, or social status. Maybe we allow ourselves to be defined by our Southern lineage, Mayflower ancestry, American Indian heritage, or other ethnic pride. Or maybe, instead of pride, there's so much shame attached to our label that it feels more like a brand—the part of town we're from, our family background, our economic condition, our lack of education, our limited job potential, our slim marriage prospects.

How about you? What labels do you wear? What can people tell about you from the name you're wearing? Are you focused on appearances and image, wearing the well-known labels of this world to give *yourself* a name? Or have others labeled you? Have you had an identity pinned on you since childhood? Do you persist in putting on the names of your past and wearing the labels of a false identity?

If so, it's time to cut out that old label. You bear the name of the Master Designer. Your label says so. Now dress yourself in Christ! You wouldn't wear anything less...and it will be a perfect fit!

*Your clothes speak even before you do.*—Jacqueline Murray

O Lord,

how I treasure the garment You made especially for me!

Thank You for Your great sacrifice,

which allows me to be wrapped in Your

very own robes of splendor and majesty.

Lord, I willingly give You my past,

my old way of thinking, and my old way of doing things.

Forgive me for hanging onto the old, dead me.

I realize that it's no longer necessary . . . and no longer flattering.

Renew my mind, Lord.

End, once and for all, any thought that I am not worthy

of the beautiful, rich garments that You Yourself have given me.

Thank You that You have clothed me in Yourself, Lord Jesus.

Thank You that I bear Your name!

Amen

# CHAPTER FOURTEEN

# A PERFECT FIT

# HAND-ME-DOWN BLESSINGS

He blesses me with every spiritual blessing...

*Praise be to the God and Father of our Lord Jesus Christ*
*who has blessed us in the heavenly realms*
*with every spiritual blessing in Christ.——Ephesians 1:3*

I GREW UP WEARING hand-me-downs. Okay, okay...they were no ordinary hand-me-downs. Bobbie Brooks, Ralph Lauren, and Villager. A pair of wheat colored, high-waisted linen pants by Geoffrey Beene, a Saks cordovan brown leather handbag, a Halston sleeveless black jersey evening dress. They were beautiful, classic—and expensive—clothes from our family's "rich" friends, Mr. and Mrs. McNeilly and their daughter, Julie.

I was awestruck by Julie. She was just a few years older than I was, but she was the epitome of elegance. I observed her every move: the way she walked, the way she wore her clothes, her perfect posture and regal manner as she sat on our red tweed sofa. Later, in the privacy of my room, I imitated each nuance, hoping that I would inherit more than just her wardrobe and praying that those beautiful clothes would mystically impart some instant sophistication.

My fourteen-year-old imagination was fertile. *What thrilling things did she do while wearing this very jacket?* I wondered. *What threshold of experience did she cross in these trousers? What exotic places has this handbag visited? Did the first blush of romance give her goose-*

*bump shivers while she was wearing this sleeveless dress?* These weren't just clothes to me. They were the literal threads of another's life, symbols of experience and passage now handed down and entrusted to me. Yes, the clothes themselves were beautiful, but they represented something more to me because of who Julie was and the very special kind of family she had.

The McNeilly family would visit us four or five times a year. Their visits were always quiet times. Whispers and soft voices mingled with sounds of iced tea glasses tinkling and sterling forks chiming softly on antique plates with lemon cake. Laughter, plentiful at our house, was present as always, but at lower volume on the days of their visits—more seen than heard.

You see, Mr. and Mrs. McNeilly were deaf.

They never heard their two daughters' beautiful voices. The girls, born able to hear, learned sign language right alongside their first utterances of "Mommy, "Daddy," and "No!" The parents were expert at reading lips, as long as whoever was speaking didn't try to *e-nun-ci-ate-to-be-un-der-stood* and mouth words like a wide-mouthed bass. Mom and I understood Mrs. McNeilly's speech quite well, so she and Julie used sign language sparingly at our house, only to clarify if one of us missed something.

I think my favorite visit with them was on a balmy day in April. Julie said something to her mother in sign language. Mrs. McNeilly signed a quick something in response. Julie signed back. Then her mother. Then Julie again. It went back and forth, fingers flying in the air faster and faster with each volley. Finally, Julie, lip quivering and eyes brimming with tears, whispered as she signed to her mother, "Well, you don't have to yell!" Then she glanced sheepishly at us, and we all burst into laughter.

Julie was kind. She was affectionate to her mother and thoughtful of mine. She treated me like I existed. She admired my Dusty

Springfield posters and listened patiently to Monkees records in my room. She was gentle and she was generous. Yes, she was pretty...long hair, I think. Funny, I don't remember her appearance as much as I remember her beauty. All I knew was that if I could be anything like her, I'd be happy.

On Julie's last visit before she went off to college, I took a mental note of the charcoal Jones of New York trousers and navy cashmere cardigan she was wearing that day and prayed that they'd be among the next batch of "goodies" she'd pass along to me. Yes, I'd luxuriate in those beautiful clothes, but my secret hope was that in wearing them I would also somehow don her mantle of kindness and grace and goodness. I was always so proud to wear Julie's hand-me-downs.

I wonder if Julie ever knew she was giving me more than just her clothes.

Just as I watched Julie, someone is watching you. Your daughter, her friends, young women you see every day at the office and the video store. They may act as if they're ignoring you, but they're watching. They're watching how you behave, what you say, the integrity you exhibit, the patience and grace and mercy you extend as you walk through your everyday life. What beautiful possessions you have to hand down to them!

*How goodness heightens beauty!*—Hannah More

# A "MRS. BROWN"
# KIND OF BEAUTY

He encourages my heart...

*May our Lord Jesus Christ... encourage your hearts and strengthen you in every good deed and word.*—2 Thessalonians 2:16–17

MY SECOND GRADE teacher, Mrs. Brown, hung the moon. With her bob of shiny, thick chestnut hair, athletic energy, and lilting laugh, she captivated her class of seven-year-olds. She was just so *different*. And so *young*. In a sea of teachers with lace collars and crowns of silver blue hair, we'd never seen anything like her. I've been blessed with wonderful teachers who've impacted me deeply, but Mrs. Brown made an immeasurable deposit in my life.

She was loving and kind to everyone in my class, but for some reason she was especially attentive to me. Maybe it was because my mom was the PTA's "dream mother," decorating bulletin boards with paper turkeys and pouring umpteen cups of Kool-Aid at snack time. Or it might have been because Mrs. Brown had two rambunctious boys at home and my ribboned pigtails and lace socks gave her a respite from frogs and trucks. But I think it was because she saw a shy little girl in the back of the class wearing her first pair of glasses.

Mrs. Brown let me stay after school and help her. I got to sort books, erase blackboards, and straighten chairs. We talked about her boys and my Brownie troop. She actually *liked* spending time with me. I felt so special!

But most meaningful of all was the day Mrs. Brown took me ice-skating. It was my first time. This Florida native had been on the Everglades but never on the ice; in fact, I'd never even seen it. We went on a muggy Saturday in August. The rink was full of skaters, and to me everyone looked like a professional. Girls my age and younger were swooshing seventy miles an hour backward, and bundled toddlers were doing straight-ankled circles in the center of the rink. I, on the other hand, was terrible. I gripped the handrail like a lifeline, hand over hand, edging my wobbly way forward.

Mrs. Brown was perfect. She made me feel as if I was doing a good job. She helped me get over my fear of falling. She encouraged me to take the risk. And when I did fall, she stayed right beside me, her smile and soothing comments helping me inch forward, forgetting the humiliation of falling and the pain of the hard ice. When I was a bit more comfortable, she held my hand tight and whispered, "Let go; I've got you."

Tentatively, I loosened my grip. We glided away from the rail, farther out onto the ice, building speed under Mrs. Brown's confident stride. Faster and faster we moved, until I could feel a cool breeze on my face. It was exhilarating! I was flying! I could do it! And Mrs. Brown knew it. She believed in me!

I've often thought about that day on the ice and what a perfect picture it is of our walk with God. He takes us places we've never gone before, places both exhilarating and terrifying. He gives us space to stand on our own and assures us that we can do what He's called us to. Then He asks us to trust Him as He takes our hand and leads us farther out, onto ground we couldn't navigate without Him. He stays close, whispers encouragement, and never gives up on us. And even if we fall, He's right there to pick us up again and take us back out onto the ice. He gives us constant encouragement through His written words and unfailing presence. And very often He sends it through someone like you or me…or Mrs. Brown.

My second-grade teacher was a gift to me, and I'm honored to say that we're still friends today. Her chestnut hair is now a crown of shiny silver, and she is as graceful and gracious as ever. Everyone in my school knew that Mrs. Brown was pretty. But to me she was—and still is—absolutely breathtaking. The generosity and love she expressed to an insecure little seven-year-old reveals her true and timeless beauty.

All of us have a "Mrs. Brown" kind of beauty just waiting to be revealed. As God Himself lifts us up and sends encouragers into our lives, we too can be the encouragers He sends to others. When we take a little time to share ourselves, when we believe in others and cheer them on, we deposit something in their lives that can never be measured.

So be extra sensitive to those around you, whether they're seven or seventy. When you spy someone who's faltering, who's a little afraid and maybe hovering at life's handrail, reach out, help her unclench her fingers, and take her for a spin on the ice. Let her feel the cool breeze on her face! It will revive her spirit and encourage her heart…and yours.

# A Cheerful Heart

He cheers my heart...

*An anxious heart weighs a man down,*
*but a kind word cheers him up.* —*Proverbs 12:25*

ARE YOU FEELING anxious? "Weighed down" is a pretty good description of how we feel when we're troubled, burdened, fearful, or worried. But how do you feel when you receive a kind word? Uplifted, lightened...cheered?

If all you did was look at my mom, you might think that she's weighed down. You would see a blind, overweight, arthritic widow in a wheelchair. But don't feel sorry for her. Emulate her. She has more life than anyone I know. Because she loves God and depends completely on Him, she has a light heart and the ability to lighten other hearts. She is a cheerful woman who spends her life cheering others. Just ask the countless people who daily benefit from her humor, her caring, and her effervescent joy.

People of all ages and interests file through Mom's door in a steady stream. This vibrant, funny, optimistic former teacher and city councilwoman is involved in more lives and encourages more people than anyone I've ever known.

And she does it all from a wheelchair in a house she hasn't left in twenty years.

Mom's degenerative arthritis and excessive weight have left her housebound, but not heartbound. Early on she made peace with her plight, and, far from bitter, her indomitable spirit just shines. Smiling and laughing through pain and tears, she refuses to talk about her own problems, but instead listens empathetically to others' woes—some bursitis here, a bum back there.

*A happy woman is one who has no cares at all; a cheerful woman is one who has cares but doesn't let them get her down.*—Beverly Sills

Mom's house is like a revolving door. She spends her days serving iced tea and pound cake to lifelong friends, ladies from the women's club, and neighborhood children. Her former kindergartners drop by to introduce their kids...and grandkids. My friends from high school swing by to reminisce about the parties where beer was never allowed, but billiards, Ping-Pong, and blaring 45s always were. My brother's political acquaintances drop by to banter about pending legislation, and Mom's friends bring her everything from bananas and aspirin to fresh-baked treats and audio books. She offers cold Cokes to the garbage men, a soft shoulder and tissues to her friends. She knows more about her mail carrier, Gail, than I do about my next-door neighbor. And when Mom sends her on her way, Gail is buoyed in spirit and staggering under a bundle of outgoing notes, all dotted with red-marker hearts.

Mom is famous for her notes. She writes dozens of them a week. They are snapshots of her day and sentiments of her heart. With just a few lines, she reminds others that they are constantly in her thoughts and prayers. She sends get wells, happy birthdays, and hurrahs for you! She conveys sympathy for loved ones who've departed and welcomes new bundles of joy. Her quickly jotted messages grace anniversaries and weddings, and her nursing-home notes cheer the ones who have no one.

These days, Mom's notes are especially cherished because she has become nearly blind. Macular degeneration has claimed her vision, but, undeterred, she places her fingers on the keys of her typewriter and relies on memory and sheer faith to hammer out her notes.

Mom has cheered many an anxious heart with her kind words. My own heart often aches for what she's missed: She's never been to California to visit me and never seen my home. She never saw her son being sworn into office at the state capitol, and she never stood with her husband on the edge of the Grand Canyon or on a glacier in Alaska. Yes, I'm sure that Mom wishes she could have gone to those places and seen those things, but she is the first to tell you that her life is rich.

My mother may be a shut-in, but she is not shut off. She may be blind, but she truly sees. She is proof that mobility of body has little to do with agility of spirit.

What encouragement, what good word, what cheer can you bring to someone who is weighed down today? *The Living Bible* says it this way, "Anxious hearts are very heavy, but a word of encouragement does wonders!" (Proverbs 12:25). And you don't even need to leave your house to do that.

*Cheerfulness, it would appear, is a matter which depends fully*
*as much on the state of things within, as on the state of things without*
*and around us.—Charlotte Brontë*

# REFLECTIONS OF HIS LOVE

"I'm showing you a new way of living. But you have to break the old patterns. Go ahead and write it down. My peace I give to you—My peace. Not as the world gives, but as I give. I will direct your ways. Be open to Me, listen for Me in all things, be attentive to My heart. The things I care about, you will care about. The things I cherish, you will cherish. A life of beauty, of peace, of surrender. I know that's what your heart yearns for. And you shall have it. Just listen for Me and to Me. I will direct the pattern of your day, your very activities, to bring honor and glory to Me and refreshment to your soul. That's the secret of life! No more being tired, overwhelmed, or stressed out—just resting in Me, skating along on top of things, refreshed, and renewed. You are in Me, as I am in you. Your very heart resonates with My heart. It beats with Mine. It is a life of pleasure, a life of devotion. A life of truth."

Lord,

thank You for the blessings of people who have

deposited their best into my life.

Thank You that I can try on their admirable traits for myself.

I pray that they will be a perfect fit.

Help me to take all the beautiful things I've received from them

and joyously pass them along to others.

Thank You for all the times You have encouraged my weary

heart and brought comfort and joy through another.

Help me to be that kind of encouragement to someone else.

Let my presence be like a cool, refreshing breeze

that brings hope and cheer to those around me.

Every day remind me that there is always

someone in need of what I possess,

including my greatest possession—You.

Amen

# CHAPTER FIFTEEN

# BEAUTY BASICS

# Sow and Reap

I reap holiness and eternal life…

*What benefit did you reap at that time from the things you are now ashamed of? Those things result in death! But now that you have been set free from sin and have become slaves to God, the benefit you reap leads to holiness, and the result is eternal life.—Romans 6:21–22*

GLORIOUS SUMMER. My favorite time of the year. The sun feels warm on my body and shines bright till the evening hours. Since my childhood in Fort Lauderdale, I've loved summer…the long, cool grass between my toes, the taste of juicy mangoes picked off our backyard trees, and the scent of moonflowers and night-blooming jasmine. I grew up just minutes from one of the world's best beaches, famous for "where the boys are" and where the mingled smells of salt and suntan lotion hover in the air like a cloud.

So it seemed especially unfair that I—pale skinned, freckle faced, and ultrasensitive to the sun—should be born into this tropical paradise tailor-made for bronzed goddesses. For years I endured the nickname "Casper." My legs were so white that you could spot me at a hundred yards on a moonless night. So in high school I determined to become one of "them"—a bronzed goddess.

Every afternoon I performed the sunbathing ritual: I aligned my chaise lounge to the exact angle of the sun, slathered on baby oil, and spritzed myself with water as Florida's 94-degree temperature and 98 percent humidity threatened me with heat stroke. And every day as I headed to the backyard sizzle-grill, my mother would say, "Nancy, honey, you'll ruin your skin."

*Hah! What does she know? She's just a mother! So what if she's a fifth-generation Floridian? Where's her tan anyway?*

So I baked and baked and baked some more. I prayed that my freckles would all grow together and blend into a glorious tan, but—alas—they never did. The brown never came. But the red did, along with more freckles and those little bubbles that come from sun poisoning. Before I went to college, I finally gave it up, but by then the damage was done.

*I don't tan—I stroke!—Woody Allen*

When I was twenty-five, I had major surgery on my face for skin cancer. I was millimeters away from disfigurement, and it rocked my world. The consequences of those summers I spent trying to bake my way to beauty taught me one of the most important lessons in my life: We reap what we sow. I just didn't believe it at the time. I ignored the warning from someone who knew better.

Today, my semiannual treks to the dermatologist for a full-body checkup under a Sherlock Holmes–sized magnifying glass remind me that there are consequences to our actions. If you're gonna play, you're gonna pay. It might be tomorrow; it might be decades. But sooner or later, if we continue to ignore wise counsel, if we take shortcuts or foolish risks, if we opt for instant gratification over wisdom, the piper comes…and we have to pay.

*Consequences are unpitying.—George Eliot*

Maybe we abuse our bodies for something other than a tan—maybe we do it for instant gratification or for a smaller dress size—yet think it will never catch up with us in terms of our health and long-term well-being. Or maybe we take shortcuts in our relationships, not investing time with our children, husband, or friends, but still expect them to always be there for us. Or maybe we imagine we can get away with not forgiving and not pay a price in bitterness or a hardening of heart down the road. Maybe we take shortcuts in our relationship with God, never getting to really know Him or the wise counsel of His Word, or even living in disobedience, and yet still believing that we'll find strength and peace during times of hardship and trouble.

Sow and reap. It's a universal principle. We can't defy it. And while reaping wrinkles is the sad result of sowing sunshine folly, damage to our skin is nothing compared to the damage we can do to hearts and spirits, either to our own or to those around us.

Recently, as my stepdaughter was heading to the pool, I heard my mother's voice coming out of my mouth, "Katie, honey, you'll ruin your skin." And then I whispered this prayer, which I'll bet Mom whispered too: *Oh, Lord, help her to heed wise counsel early in life—especially from You.*

*Their mothers had finally caught up to them and been proven right. There were consequences after all; but they were the consequences to things you didn't even know you'd done.*—Margaret Atwood

# MARK MY WORDS

I speak words of life to others…

*The tongue that brings healing is a tree of life,*
*but a deceitful tongue crushes the spirit.* —*Proverbs 15:4*

THE COSMETICS COUNTER at Neiman Marcus was jammed. It was noontime, and I just wanted to slip in, buy a lipstick, and be on my way. But the place was crawling with gals all wanting to do the same thing. I took my position at the counter and waited…and watched. One young would-be starlet, sporting a micromini and bee-stung lips fresh from the plastic surgeon's office, was huffy with the clerk and everyone else within earshot. The irony struck me: Her ugly behavior cancelled out all her surgical efforts to look pretty.

Then I glanced down the counter and saw a mom trying on countless nuanced shades of fuschia lipgloss while her five-year-old son waited by her side. He was patient for a few minutes, and then he became squirmy and a little whiny. *He's hungry,* I thought—and empathized as I felt my own tummy growl for some lunch. After a minute or two of his repeated pleas of "Can we goooo now, please?" his mom had finally had it. She pushed her collection of fuschias aside and grabbed him by the forearm, nearly yanking his shoulder from its socket. "Shut up! Mommy's trying to buy something to make her look pretty. Now straighten up, or I'll spank you in front of everyone!"

*You want to look pretty?* I thought. *Unclenching your teeth might be the ticket. Poor kid. When he grows up, he'll wonder why he hates pink lipstick.*

My attention was gradually diverted from that scene by the two women standing next to me, whose voices got louder and louder as they peppered their conversation with gossip. They prattled on, speaking foolishness and gushing folly as they gave each other the lowdown on everyone they knew. I felt relieved that I'd never met them, so I wasn't on their list. I had to bite my lip to keep from smiling when one said, "I don't know why they're so mad at me. I never say anything about anyone!"

*Violence of the tongue is very real—
sharper than any knife.—Mother Teresa*

That day at the lipstick counter I saw the tremendous power of our lips. We put on lipgloss, but forget to smooth our conversation. We make our lips bright with lipstick, but forget to smile. We obsess over how our lips look and then speak too much, too quickly, too harshly. The book of Proverbs is full of counsel about our lips: "The tongue has the power of life and death, and those who love it will eat its fruit" (Proverbs 18:21). And "The lips of the wise spread knowledge; not so the hearts of fools" (Proverbs 15:7).

The heart, it seems, is the heart of the matter. You see, the root issue isn't really the lips at all—it's the heart. Jesus said, "Out of the overflow of the heart the mouth speaks" (Matthew 12:34). We can't change what comes from our lips unless we change our hearts. No matter how much we may try to speak wisely, kindly, or lovingly, in our own effort it will only be our own effort. We can't change from the outside in. But Christ can change us from the inside out. The more of Him we have, the more like Him we behave, in our attitudes, actions…and speech. And as He transforms us, Jesus says, "The good man brings good things out of the good stored up in him" (Matthew 12:35).

We've all been at the receiving end of harsh or thoughtless words. Sometimes it takes only a second to inflict deep wounds, but it might take years for them to heal. We've seen how God heals us of the words spoken to and about us that have caused us pain. Now it's up to us to guard our own tongues, so that the things we say will bring no harm to others.

The Lord reminds us that "men will have to give account on the day of judgment for every careless word they have spoken. For by your words you will be acquitted, and by your words you will be condemned" (Matthew 12:36–37). Never underestimate the importance of your lips. There's a lot of power there—for good and evil.

That day at the makeup counter I was reminded of what the psalmist said: "A wise man's heart guides his mouth, and his lips promote instruction" (Proverbs 16:23). And every day as I put on my new lipstick, I offer a silent prayer, as he did: "May the words of my mouth and the meditation of my heart be pleasing in your sight, O LORD" (Psalm 19:14).

*A word is dead when it is said, some say.*
*I say it just begins to live that day.*—Emily Dickinson

# THE EYES OF MY HEART

He satisfies my hunger with good things...

*Let them give thanks to the Lord for his unfailing love and his wonderful deeds for men, for he satisfies the thirsty and fills the hungry with good things.*—*Psalm 107:8–9*

Psssst.

You can be honest. Nobody's listening. It's just you and me...and, well...God.

Do you ever feel this way? You look around and all you see are the things you *don't* have: the career and love life you've dreamed of that haven't happened, the things you want to buy and can't afford, the Jabez blessings everyone but you seems to be enjoying.

Well, I've felt like that more than once. One day I realized that I was becoming exhausted—emotionally, physically, and spiritually—from thinking about and scrambling after what I *didn't* have. It seemed that the more I focused on what was lacking in my life, the more anxious, bitter, and depressed I became; and the more anxious and depressed I got, the more I focused on the lack. It was a vicious cycle.

Then one day God invaded my mind. *You need to know Me better,* He whispered softly. *Pray Paul's prayer to the Ephesians. Open your eyes.*

In Ephesians 1:17–19, I saw where God was leading me, so I prayed Paul's prayer for myself:

I keep asking that You, the God of our Lord Jesus Christ, the glorious Father, will give me the Spirit of wisdom and revelation, so that I may know You better. I pray also that the eyes of my heart may be enlightened in order that I may know the hope to which You have called me, the riches of Your glorious inheritance in the saints, and Your incomparably great power for us who believe.

*The eyes of my eyes are opened.*——e. e. cummings

And an amazing thing happened—the eyes of my heart *were* enlightened. They were opened. It was as if I was shaken awake from a deep, self-centered sleep. For the first time in a long time, I began to look at my life with new eyes, and I saw how much I had to be grateful for. I was humbled as I realized what amazing riches I had in my life, and I mourned the fact that I had taken so much abundance for granted. How could I keep praying "more, Lord, *more,*" when I didn't even appreciate what I already had?

To build my attitude of gratitude, I made a list of my life's blessings: a relationship with Christ, a loving husband, a wonderful family, good health, dear and faithful friends, a peaceful home, sweet dogs to cuddle, work I love, our dream of a ranch coming true....

Then I added the blessings in the past that paved the way for what I now enjoy: my parents' love and sacrifices, early encouragers and mentors, my education, my career, my life experiences and challenges, even the pain and difficulties that have shaped who I am today.

As my list grew, I became overwhelmed with gratitude to God. I began giving thanks for everything: the vine of brilliant purple morning glories, my husband's healing hugs, the first whiff of coffee in the morning, the painting in my living room that always nourishes my soul, the juicy peaches from our orchard, the comical antics of the kittens in the barn, my mother's cheerful voice and laughter. I began to appreciate the small but powerful gifts of the everyday. The eyes of my heart were enlightened, and I saw some of the riches of my glorious inheritance in the saints. As I looked at my list, I realized that I was a very rich woman indeed.

*Never lose an opportunity of seeing anything that is beautiful;*
*for beauty is God's handwriting—a wayside sacrament.*
*Welcome it in every fair face, in every fair sky, in every fair flower,*
*and thank God for it as a cup of blessing.—Ralph Waldo Emerson*

Open your eyes and heart and take another look at your own life. Do you have a home to sleep in, food on your table, friends and family you love and who love you, clothes to wear, music and beauty and sights that delight you, a dream that excites you? Then stop—right now—and give thanks. Let gratitude overflow in your heart.

Let's satisfy our hunger for the "good life" that we think others lead by recognizing the many blessings that already exist in our own lives. And then let's offer God the gift of our grateful hearts, "always giving thanks to God the Father for everything, in the name of our Lord Jesus Christ" (Ephesians 5:20).

There's nothing more basic to beauty than that!

*There shall be eternal summer in the grateful heart.—Celia Thaxter*

Father,

forgive me for thinking that there are

no consequences for my choices.

Keep me—and those I love—from actions

today that will harm our tomorrows.

Help me to sow what is good and right and true in my life.

Help me to guard my lips.

Remind me that the words of my mouth can bring life—

or death—to others.

Let my mouth be a fountain of wisdom,

and my words like a honeycomb,

sweet to the soul and healing to the bones.

Thank You for all the many blessings of my life, Lord.

Forgive my lack of gratitude.

Open the eyes of my understanding to

see how rich You have made me.

Amen

# CHAPTER SIXTEEN

# ETERNAL PLEASURES

# WHAT ARE YOU DOING?

He makes me glad with the joy of His presence…

*Surely you have granted him eternal blessings
and made him glad with the joy of your presence.——Psalm 21:6*

I'VE NEVER KNOWN anyone who could do as much as my friend Gayle. Unless maybe it's me. Or how about…you?

Gayle is an extremely successful businesswoman and former president of a major clothing manufacturing company. She serves on several foundations and boards and personally ministers to a large number of people every week. She is accomplished, capable, and busy, busy, busy.

Gayle and I pray together every week, and our prayer time lately has been fascinating because one of the things the Lord is addressing is His desire to change the "performance mentality" we both have. We have trouble allowing ourselves time for fun or relaxation. We feel that we always need to be *doing* something. If we're not being "productive," we feel guilty. We're asking the Lord to heal us of that need, perhaps that insecurity, or maybe even that fear, which drives us to have to *do* and doesn't allow us to just *be*.

Are you anything like us? (Want to join our prayer time?) As we talked and prayed about it, we realized that this kind of thinking is learned at an early age and that we'd both learned it well. I was reminded of my family as I was growing up. Ours was always a busy, efficient, productive household, full of activity and high achievers. No bunch of slackers at the Stafford house!

My mother was the first female elected official in our city, president of the Women's Club, and a full-time teacher who took care of a house full of kindergartners until their mothers picked them up at five o'clock every day. My father spent every waking hour he wasn't at the office building our house and doing various and sundry projects in his workshop. My brother, Tracy, was our church's youth pastor in high school and the national president of his college fraternity. After he became a lawyer, he served as a city councilman, then as mayor, and then as a state legislator. Whew…my head hurts…I need an aspirin just thinking about it!

The question "What are you doing?" was asked a lot around our house, not in an accusatory way, but with the distinct expectation that we would most certainly be doing something pretty worthwhile and constructive. Now, there's nothing wrong with accomplishing things. In fact, we will achieve little of value in our lives if we don't *do*. I'm talking about having an excessive need to *do* in order to feel good about ourselves and finding it difficult to rest and just *be*.

Even now, when my husband enters the room and innocently asks me what I'm doing, I get an immediate pang of guilt…or irritation. I feel as though I need to be doing something productive, something important, and I feel delinquent if I'm sitting down answering e-mail or reading a book. I have to fight my tendency to leap up and start filing or writing checks! But as I pray about this, the Lord is making inroads in my old patterns of behavior. He's changing the way I think. So now when my husband asks, "What are you doing?" I can say, "Not much" or "Just reading," without feeling guilty or lunging for the laundry basket.

How about you? Is it hard for you to just *be*? In our prayer time,

Gayle and I realized that much of our problem was our view of God. We tended to see Him as a joyless taskmaster who looked at us approvingly only if we were doing work, work, work. We realized that we were missing a huge part of the nature and beauty of God: His grace. We thought we had understood it. But we realized that, even though we knew it in our minds in a theological sense, our hearts were struggling with the misconception that we still somehow had to earn God's love and approval. We were still finding our feelings of significance and worth in our activities and achievements, not wholly in God's acceptance of us by His grace.

The apostle Paul must have seen a lot of this faulty thinking, because he went out of his way to impress upon us that we are saved by grace, not works. None of us can do anything to earn it or take credit for it. It's purely a gift of God. Maybe Paul realized what constant uncertainty we'd live in if we thought we had to earn God's love. Maybe he knew that in the times we fail God, in the times we aren't *doing* well or *doing* what we should or think we should, we would feel completely unloved, unaccepted, or unworthy. So he reminded us:

> When the kindness and love of God our Savior appeared,
> he saved us, not because of righteous things we had *done,*
> but because of his mercy. He saved us through the washing
> of rebirth and renewal by the Holy Spirit, whom he
> poured out on us generously through Jesus Christ our
> Savior, so that, having been justified by his grace, we
> might become heirs having the hope of eternal life.
> TITUS 3:4–7, EMPHASIS ADDED

As Gayle and I repented of our wrong thinking, we asked God to change our perception and knowledge of Him. *Show me who You really are, Lord!* I prayed. *Give me a way to understand Your grace. I want to know You as You really are.*

Immediately a picture of a huge field of yellow daisies came to my mind. Then Jesus' head popped up. He was lying on His back in the daisies.

He grinned. "I'm just lying here looking."

Then I saw Him lying on a cloud, then in the hammock, then on my veranda writing on my laptop computer, then working out in an exercise class, then on a horse on the trail.

"I'm everywhere you want to be. I am in all the true pleasures of life. You will find Me there as much as you will find Me in the drudgery."

Then He got up and waved me over to Him, and we played leapfrog across the field! At that moment I grasped the joy and freedom that comes from *being* a cherished daughter of God, not just *doing* the Christian life.

"You have permission to enjoy your life," He said slowly and distinctly. "I give you permission."

He gives you permission too.

What's your perception of God? Do you see Him as a taskmaster or a joymaster? Is there a part of you that can't enjoy the pleasures of your life because of your misconception of God and His grace? Do you still feel you have to earn His love, that it's what you *do* that makes Him accept you?

Theologian Karl Barth, after writing thousands of pages of *Church Dogmatics,* arrived at this simple definition of God: He is "the One who loves." Once, at a press conference crowded with students and scholars, someone asked him, "Dr. Barth, what is the most profound truth you have learned in your studies?" Without hesitation he replied, "Jesus loves me, this I know, for the Bible tells me so." In *What's So Amazing About Grace,* Philip Yancey says that grace means there is nothing we can do to make God love us more and nothing we can do to make God love us less.[24]

Now I'm beginning to understand why Jesus said, "I praise you, Father, Lord of heaven and earth, because you have hidden these things from the wise and learned, and revealed them to little children. Yes, Father, for this was your good pleasure" (Matthew 11:25–26). And again, "Let the little children come to me, and do not hinder them, for the kingdom of heaven belongs to such as these" (Matthew 19:14).

I want to be like one of the little children, scurrying up onto Jesus' lap. I want to play leapfrog, and patty-cake, and tag. I want to understand the freedom of His grace and the beauty and delight of His love. I want to nestle into His heart and listen to Him whisper words of love and acceptance. I want to just *be* with Him.

C. S. Lewis wrote, "The Scotch catechism says that man's chief end is 'to glorify God and enjoy Him forever.' But we shall then know that these are the same thing. Fully to enjoy is to glorify. In commanding us to glorify Him, God is inviting us to enjoy Him."[25]

In Psalm 21:6, David praises God for what He's done for the king, saying, "Surely you have granted him eternal blessings and made him glad with the joy of your presence." Can you imagine Him taking delight in your fun, enjoying your company, and just wanting to be with you? He does. When God asks, "What are you doing?" He means, "Won't you come out and be with Me? Can you come out and play?"

*Too many people, too many demands, too much to do; competent, busy, hurrying people—it just isn't living at all.—Anne Morrow Lindbergh*

# THE STRIKING BEAUTY
## OF BOWLING

He gives me eternal pleasures at His right hand...

*You will fill me with joy in your presence,
with eternal pleasures at your right hand.—Psalm 16:11*

NOT LONG AGO I was in Tucson, Arizona. My hotel was over-flowing with women. There were women everywhere, thousands of them—women of every age, every size, every shape. They were from all over the world, from Stockholm, Sweden, to Vancouver, B.C., to Hainesville, Georgia. And all of them were laughing and chatting, delighted to have come together to share the one thing they all had in common—bowling!

It was the annual Women's International Bowling Championship. Thirtysomethings to seventy-year-olds played on the same team, competing yet supporting one another as teammates, involved in physical activity as well as one another's lives, excelling in what they were good at but also being challenged to do better.

And you know what? All of these women were extremely attractive. They weren't all wearing the latest trends in makeup colors, a few were zealously hanging onto their lacquered beehives, and they weren't all a size eight—in fact, few were. But each had a bounce in her step, a smile on her face, and a ready laugh that was absolutely contagious. They had a confidence that comes from going and doing…and being.

I was impressed.

And I felt a connection with these ladies, though I haven't played the game since the mandatory semester of bowling in Miss Howard's ninth-grade gym class, when I was dubbed the "Gutter Queen" and, mortified, spent the entire term trying to explain to everyone that it was purely a reference to my sports prowess.

I felt a kinship with these lady bowlers because no matter where we live or how old we are or what we do for a living, we all need something that brings enjoyment to our lives, something we can succeed at, something we just plain love doing.

> *I pray you.… Your play needs no excuse. Never excuse.*—*William Shakespeare*

For some of us, it won't be bowling. There are plenty of options. My friend Debi joined a reading club. My neighbor Jeanne, a recent widow, goes on Elderhostel adventures and just got back from a photography odyssey through Yosemite National Park. My pal Larry took a six-week Asian cooking class. My friend Kimberly takes a stand-up comedy class in the evenings after teaching an eighth-grade class all day. You could take a course on Postimpressionist art, or Shakespeare, or Puccini's operas. How about swing-dancing classes, fishing or pottery, or archery or tennis lessons at the local recreation center? The possibilities are endless. Let your imagination run wild.

If you aren't really sure what kinds of things turn you on, now's the time to find out. Look for things that excite your imagination, sharpen your intelligence, challenge your body, open you up to new experiences, and put you in touch with stimulating, interesting people. Is there a subject you'd like to know more about? A place you'd like to visit? Something you've wanted to do, but just never got around to it? Give it a whirl, just for the fun of it. Put your perfectionism aside and dive right in. It doesn't matter how bad you are at it, you'll get better. Don't be shy, don't be scared, and don't put it off. If you wait until you "have the time," it'll never happen. As busy as our lives are, we have to *make* time for doing the things we enjoy.

I know what you're thinking. But try to tune out those competing voices that say, "It's not constructive; it's self-indulgent." Of course it is! That's the beauty! You're discovering a creative, passionate, vital part of yourself that has lain dormant far too long. It's a *hunger* for expression and fun that God Himself put in you. He gave us our talents and desires, and when we embrace and enjoy them, we experience His presence and His pleasure.

> *A little of what you fancy*
> *does you good.* — Marie Lloyd

That day in Tucson I was reminded of a lot. Those lovely ladies of the bowling league proved, once again, that the best beauty advice isn't about the latest beauty products and has nothing to do with anything you buy and apply. It has to do with the inner radiance that comes from a tended-to spirit and joy-filled experiences. Being active and involved in hobbies, sports, and especially in other people, increases your confidence and brings unexpected joy to your life. You feel freer, happier, and more fulfilled. And that has a powerful impact on your entire life—your work, your friends, and especially your family. They'll say, "Wow! What happened to you? You look absolutely radiant!"

See? And I'll bet it never dawned on you that bowling could be a beauty tip. But ya know, if worn with just the right socks, those shoes can make a *fabulous* fashion statement!

*Taking joy in life is a woman's*
*best cosmetic.*—Rosalind Russell

# REFLECTIONS OF HIS LOVE

I'm feeling worn out, overwhelmed, resentful.

"You're afraid," God says. "Afraid of having a dreary life with no pleasure—just work and service and drudgery."

*Yes,* I admit, tears springing to my eyes.

"Let Me in to reorder things. Let Me show you the pleasures of My right hand. The pleasure is not where you think. The pleasure is in experiencing life, being attuned, being vibrant and vital—but not to the mundane—to Me."

Then I had a picture in my mind: As I stepped onto a small stepladder, my head and neck rose through a dense, low cloud bank. Above the cloud layer I could see the crystal blue sky and smell the crisp air and feel the cool breeze. All my senses were heightened.

Jesus was steadying me, so I could relax and enjoy all the beauty. Suddenly, I noticed…He was holding me by His right hand. Pleasures to share with me! He who stands at the right hand of the Father is my sustainer, my protector, and my eternal pleasure.

Lord,

thank You that You are a God of joy and delight!

Thank You that You find pleasure in giving me pleasure!

Help me to understand that part of You better, Lord.

Forgive me for misjudging You,

for not seeing Your goodness and grace,

for not understanding that You are the creator

of all things, including my joy.

With gratitude I receive all You have given me.

Help me relish all the pleasures of Your right hand,

especially the pleasure of just being with You.

Help me to understand that my being,

my doing, and all my delights

are glorifying to You!

Amen

# CHAPTER SEVENTEEN

# FINISHING TOUCHES

# A Sweet Perfume

He makes me the fragrance of life...

*But thanks be to God, who...through us spreads everywhere the fragrance of the knowledge of him.—2 Corinthians 2:14*

THE SUMMER AIR is thick with fragrance...hickory-smoke barbecues, drippy peaches, fresh-mowed lawns, salty air. Intoxicating smells of jasmine, rose, and gardenia hang heavy in the air like an invisible blanket. Whiffs of peanut butter from picnic baskets, spray starch, and cocoa butter float on a breeze and flit teasingly by during the sultry, steamy days of summer. Fragrance has the power to move us, soothe us, stir us, ignite us.

The barest hint of a scent wafts past, carrying with it a memory. Is that Old Spice? *Boom!* Suddenly, I'm sitting on my daddy's lap after work, his strong arms cradling me, my head buried under his whiskery five o'clock chin, breathing deep the safe, sweet, lingering fragrance of my dear dad. The memory is sudden and rich. My hot tears and tight throat remind me how much I still miss him since his death. I feel the pain of loss mingled with joy and gratitude for having been his daughter.

Scents are powerful. They can take us to places remembered or to those only imagined. They can change the very atmosphere in a room: lavender soothes, peppermint stimulates, lemon refreshes.

Fragrance can usher in sleep and lighten our mood. And as Proverbs 27:9 says, "Perfume and incense bring joy to the heart."

Our very lives can be a fragrant offering, a sweet-smelling scent, pleasing to God and a blessing to others. We can experience the fragrance of God as He pours Himself into us, and we can be His fragrance wherever we go—an aroma of His life.

Too often we're unaware that our fragrance can bless people. But as we move through their world in gentleness, mercy, and loving-kindness, we can leave behind a soft, beautiful, unforgettable trace of ourselves and of God—a fragrance that lingers. Like my dad.

What kind of fragrance are you to others? Do your words, actions, and attitudes emit a pleasing aroma, sweet and refreshing? Today, let God use you to spread His essence, His fragrance—the fragrance of life.

# THE PERFECT PURSE

### He gives me treasure in heaven…

*"Provide purses for yourselves that will not wear out, a treasure
in heaven that will not be exhausted, where no thief comes near
and no moth destroys. For where your treasure is,
there your heart will be also."* —Luke 12:33–34

I NEEDED A new purse. I'd gotten these great little silver gray sandals, and all my bags were either black or brown, roomy daytime
catchalls or tiny evening thingies. I saw a cute bag by Nine West in
a magazine and thought, *Mmm, maybe I'll get that one.* I called my
friend Holly and asked her to go shopping with me. We'd have
lunch, catch up, and peruse the mall. Holly already had plans for the
morning and was flying out the door. She invited me to go with her.
We'd shop afterwards.

I picked her up, and as she scrambled into my car, her purse
caught my eye. I guess I had handbags on the brain. I chuckled to
myself, because in the five years I'd known her, it's the only purse I'd
ever seen her carry. It was a simple, black leather shoulder bag, limp
soft and shiny smooth from wear. The dye had rubbed off the bottom
right corner. The buckle was dull, and a few stitches were frayed on the
strap. Then and there I decided that Holly definitely needed a new
purse too.

*It's a good thing I came today. I'm glad I can help her. Must be a
God thing.*

I was excited about going to the mall. Holly was more excited about where we were going first. Oh, I go there myself from time to time, but I didn't want to that day. I just wanted to see Holly. And shop. I really needed that purse. So we'd go for a little while, and then we could hit the mall on the way back.

We headed downtown. Really downtown. Watts.

The building was already bulging with people. It was old and musty, cold and echoey. The smell of stale sweat and urine mingled with pot roast, sheet cake, and coffee. I carefully tucked my purse in a corner, trying to hide it under a few stowed jackets.

*Ya never know—we're in a bad area, and we don't really know any of these people. I wish I'd left my wallet in the car.*

Holly came right behind me and tossed her purse on the top of the pile.

*Careless. She'll be sorry.*

Then she rolled up her sleeves. Fifty people were already waiting in the food line.

Holly dished out carrots and peas, comfort and mercy. Along with lemonade, she poured out compassion. She served sheet cake and kindness, coffee and consideration. Her generous offers of a second helping were gracious pictures of a second chance. She looked everyone in the eye as she served each one, her smile and soothing voice a true shelter from the cold. She handed steaming plates of food to nourish their bellies and dignity and courtesy to feed their souls.

Then she handed out blankets and sneakers, tiny soaps, combs, and toothbrushes. She made sure that babies had waterproof diapers and their parents had weatherproof parkas. Rifling through mountains of clothes to find warm fuzzy socks, she spied a sweater that matched someone's eyes. She helped one dapper man find a green sports jacket to go with his chartreuse sweatpants. She doled out toys and laughter to the children, honor and respect to the adults. She sat with them, listened to them, touched them, prayed with them. She was extravagant in tenderness and kindness and attention. She heaped on grace and blessing. She lavished them with love.

She reminded me of Jesus.

After the Lord called His twelve disciples, He sent them out with the following instructions: "As you go, preach this message: 'The kingdom of heaven is near.'... Freely you have received, freely give. Do not take along any gold or silver or copper in your belts; *take no bag for the journey,* or extra tunic, or sandals or a staff" (Matthew 10:7–10, emphasis added). My friend Holly was living the gospel. She was bringing the kingdom of heaven near.

> *Do not let the bread of the hungry mildew in your larder!*
> *Do not let moths eat the poor man's cloak.*
> *Do not store the shoes of the barefoot.*
> *Do not hoard the money of the needy.*
> *Things you possess in too great abundance belong to*
> *the poor and not to you.*—Christine de Pisan

I thought of the words of the prophet Haggai, words that convict us today as much as they did the nation of Israel five hundred years before Christ:

"Give careful thought to your ways. You have planted much, but have harvested little. You eat, but never have enough. You drink, but never have your fill. You put on clothes, but are not warm. You earn wages, only to put them in a purse with holes in it.... You expected much, but see, it turned out to be little. What you brought home,

I blew away. Why?… Because of my house, which remains
a ruin, while each of you is busy with his own house."
HAGGAI 1:5–6, 9

That day I realized that I'd been awfully busy building my own
house. How about you? Have you been busy building your own
house, living comfortably and safely behind the four walls of your
life, taking care of your own needs, making sure you have warm
clothes, good food—maybe even a new purse—despite the obvious
needs of others? Or are you building God's house?

Building God's house today has nothing to do with bricks and
mortar. Building God's house means serving Christ, following in His
footsteps, doing what He did, and fulfilling the gospel by preaching
good news to the poor, opening the eyes of the blind to the truth of
Christ, and proclaiming freedom for prisoners and release for the
oppressed. Just as in Haggai's day, when we give priority to God and
His house, we are blessed. We build up treasure in heaven that
neither moth nor rust can destroy and that thieves can never steal.
And one day:

> The King will say to those on his right, "Enter, you who
> are blessed by my Father! Take what's coming to you in
> this kingdom. It's been ready for you since the world's
> foundation. And here's why:
>
> > I was hungry and you fed me,
> > I was thirsty and you gave me a drink,
> > I was homeless and you gave me a room,
> > I was shivering and you gave me clothes,
> > I was sick and you stopped to visit,
> > I was in prison and you came to me."

Then those "sheep" are going to say, "Master, what are you talking about? When did we ever see you hungry and feed you, thirsty and give you a drink? And when did we ever see you sick or in prison and come to you?" Then the King will say, "I'm telling the solemn truth: Whenever you did one of these things to someone overlooked or ignored, that was me—you did it to me."

MATTHEW 25:24–40, THE MESSAGE

As we were leaving, Holly gathered up her handbag and slung it over her shoulder. Again her purse caught my eye. No, it was nothing to look at on the outside, still old and worn and frayed. But this time its beauty captivated me. I remembered the words of Jesus: "Sell your possessions and give to the poor. Provide purses for yourselves that will not wear out, a treasure in heaven that will not be exhausted, where no thief comes near and no moth destroys. For where your treasure is, there your heart will be also" (Luke 12:33–34).

Holly had a purse that will never wear out, one filled with infinite treasure that God was keeping for her in heaven. And I wanted one just like it.

I cancelled my shopping trip.

*Man may dismiss compassion from his heart, but God never will.—William Cowper*

# REFLECTIONS OF HIS LOVE

_Lord, I've asked You to help me say no to the things I "consume"—food, shopping, busyness, distractions, anxious thoughts. Lately it seems not a day goes by that I don't buy things…some necessary, but some not. So I want to try, Lord, with Your help, a fast on consuming goods. No clothes, no shopping, no purchasing what I don't need. The distraction is intense, and the time spent away from home to do it—and away from what I need to be doing—is too destructive. I'm doing exactly what the enemy wants._

_So God, I come to You broken—no sense of my own capability, no confidence in myself to do much of anything—and I stand on Your Word that I can do all things through Christ who strengthens me. And I pray that You will use this time of weakness and failure in my life, this time of need in every area—obedience, discipline, finances, vision for the future—to bring me to a new depth of dependency and intimacy._

_So Lord, rather than consume, I choose to fast. Rather than take in for myself, I choose to expend my energies and time for others. Help me, Holy Spirit, in this fast. Increase Your power and presence in my life as I give You access. I submit myself to You for Your mercy. Change me, Lord._

# A CROWNING GLORY

He crowns me with splendor...

*You will be a crown of splendor in the Lord's hand,*
*a royal diadem in the hand of your God.*—*Isaiah 62:3*

KEEPING A CROWN on your head is a lot like putting an idol—or yourself—on a pedestal. They both have a tendency to fall off.

I wore a literal crown for a year. Well, not every day for a whole year like a real queen—just when I attended special functions, spoke at events, emceed local pageants, or otherwise represented my state as America's queen reigning in the province of Florida. Mind you, I said *America,* not *U.S.A.* I was in the *real* pageant—the Miss *America* pageant—as in "*America* the Beautiful," "God Bless *America,*" "Bye-Bye Miss *American* Pie." Not that I'm funny about it or anything....

I wore the Miss Florida crown with pride, honor, and great pleasure. I just had a tough time keeping the thing on. Maybe it had something to do with the shape of my head.

I didn't win the title of Miss America, but my picture did manage to make the front page of the newspapers the morning after the pageant. You see, in order for the papers to pull the winner's photo in time for the early edition, all fifty women are lined up the day of the pageant, and, one after another in alphabetical order and at breakneck speed, each contestant is photographed in full Miss

America regalia. Each one dons the crown and grasps the scepter for her ten seconds of glory before the props are snatched away and the crown is plopped onto the next state's head. The photographer has it down to a science. Shooting the entire nation doesn't take him more than fifteen minutes, tops. The crown is plopped on a head, and as soon as it stops wobbling and settles, the sequence begins: Plop…flash…"Thank You!"…snatch…"Next!"…plop…and so on down the line.

No sooner had they plopped the crown on my head than it began to slip and slide on my newly conditioned hair. I started to say, "Wait a second, please," but the photographer's assistant said, "It's fine; it's fine. Leave it alone!" But the thought of this "sacred" headgear crashing to the ground was too much, and reflexively my hand flew up to catch the falling crown, when…. Plop…flash…"Thank You!"…snatch…"Next!"

My "almost Miss America" picture shows the crown forever frozen in midair, my hand up and fingers spread clawlike to catch it, my shocked face contorted into a half laugh, half silent scream. The good news is that it was a perfect catch. Not a rhinestone was lost.

The day after the pageant more newspapers ran that picture of me and my toppling crown than they did the photo of Miss America. I may not have won, but I was notorious in all fifty states. I guess that means…something.

*Uneasy lies the head that wears a crown.*—William Shakespeare

Over the years I've thought some about the year I wore a crown. But I've thought a lot more about the one that still awaits me. I can identify with what Paul told the believers in Rome: "Everyone who competes in the games goes into strict training. They do it to get a crown that will not last; but we do it to get a crown that will last forever" (1 Corinthians 9:25). When I was getting ready to compete in the pageant, there *was* some strict training—in piano, at least—but now I'm in training for something else: "the crown of righteousness, which the Lord, the righteous Judge, will award to me on that day—and not only to me, but also to all who have longed for his appearing" (2 Timothy 4:8).

In pageants it's common to hear the phrase "everyone's a winner," even though only one woman walks away with the prize. But in the kingdom of God all of us who know Him will get a crown. And this crown will never be snatched away. The only time ours will come off is when we cast it at His feet. One glorious day there will be a multitude of us in heaven laying our crowns before God's throne and crying, "Worthy is the Lamb, who was slain, to receive power and wealth and wisdom and strength and honor and glory and praise!" (Revelation 5:12).

Lord,

I so desire to be a pleasing fragrance to

You and to those around me.

Let my words, my actions, and my attitudes

be a pleasing aroma, sweet and refreshing.

Give me an extravagant heart!

Forgive me for my self-centeredness.

Help me to think less of myself and more of others.

I so want a purse filled with the treasures that You value.

Thank You that You have given me a

crown of beauty instead of ashes.

May I always be a crown of splendor in Your hands.

And though You crown me Your own, I choose, Lord,

to cast my crown at Your feet in worship and adoration.

You are worthy, my Lord and God and King,

to receive glory and honor and power.

Amen

# A NEW MIRROR

FOR TOO LONG we've been looking in the wrong mirror. We've been seeing ourselves the way others see us, not the way God sees us. It's just like looking in a mirror at a funhouse. When we look at others to see who we are, we get a distorted view, and when we act as if the image is true, we're deceived. True beauty is so much more than mere physical appearance.

When we compare ourselves to media images, we never really measure up. When we live our lives to win the approval and acceptance of others, we never really feel secure. And when we allow the pain of the past to rule the present and future, we never really live in freedom.

The popular girl thinks that her acceptance is proof of her personhood, so when she is rejected, her identity disappears. The successful career woman thinks that her worth lies in her accomplishments, so when she fails, she feels worthless. The wife and mother thinks that her life consists of only that, so when her kids go off to college or her husband decides to leave her, she dies inside.

*mir • ror:*

*anything that faithfully reflects or gives a true picture of something else*

We all need an accurate picture of the one staring back at us in the mirror. We have to know what God says about us. Don't misjudge yourself. Don't confuse *yourself* with your appearance, with your work, with your family, or with your acceptance in our culture or society. Real beauty isn't determined by popular culture. It isn't found on the pages of glossy magazines or reflected in media images…or even in the mirror of your own compact. Your value isn't measured by youth or thinness or fashion. And your acceptance today isn't determined by your mistakes of yesterday or marred by the pain of your past.

No…you won't find your beauty, value, and acceptance in any of those things. But you will find them in the pages of an ancient Book, where the Creator of the universe tells you over and over again who you really are, how valuable you are to Him, and how much He loves you and accepts you. Only through the pages of the Book can you discover who you are and what true beauty looks like.

The Bible is full of God's opinion of you. Throughout it, He tells you how much He treasures you and who He has made you to be. Use the Scriptures I've given you in this book and search for other passages in the Bible that tell you who the Lord is and who you are because of what Jesus has done. Speak the Scriptures aloud and meditate on their truth. Let their power penetrate to your heart. Commit them to memory. Daily renew your mind and your spirit with their truths.

As you begin to truly grasp how much God loves you and how much He has done for you—and you begin to live in that freedom and wholeness and acceptance—you become who you were meant to be all along. You begin to see yourself reflected in the mirror of God's Word.

That's beauty by the Book!

*The soul, by an instinct stronger than reason,*
*ever associates beauty with truth.—Henry Theodore Tuckerman*

Lord,

You are the way, You are the truth, You are the life.

You are Beauty itself.

I am enthralled by You.

You have taken away the veil of deception.

You have shown me the truth of who I am,

and day by day You are transforming me into Your likeness.

May my life always reflect You in ever-increasing glory.

May You always be enthralled by my beauty!

Amen

# In the Mirror of God's Word, I See...

| | |
|---|---|
| 1 Samuel 12:22 | I am His own. |
| 1 Samuel 16:7 | He sees my heart. |
| 2 Kings 20:5 | He heals me. |
| 1 Chronicles 28:8 | I will pass on an inheritance. |
| Job 23:10 | He knows the way that I take. |
| Psalm 16:11 | He gives me eternal pleasures at His right hand. |
| Psalm 21:6 | He makes me glad with the joy of His presence. |
| Psalm 27:4 | I will gaze upon the beauty of the Lord forever. |
| Psalm 27:10 | He will never forsake me. |
| Psalm 34:18 | He is near me. |
| Psalm 45:11 | He is enthralled by my beauty. |
| Psalm 91:14 | He rescues me. |
| Psalm 103:4 | He crowns me with love and compassion. |
| Psalm 107:9 | He satisfies my hunger with good things. |
| Psalm 139:14 | I am wonderfully made. |
| Proverbs 12:25 | He cheers my heart. |
| Proverbs 15:4 | I speak words of life to others. |
| Song of Songs 7:10 | I belong to Him. |
| Isaiah 41:18 | He makes my wilderness like Eden. |

| | |
|---|---|
| ISAIAH 53:4 | He bears my pain. |
| ISAIAH 61:3 | He gives me a crown of beauty instead of ashes. |
| ISAIAH 61:10 | He wraps me in a robe of righteousness. |
| ISAIAH 62:2 | He calls me by a new name. |
| ISAIAH 62:3 | He crowns me with splendor. |
| ISAIAH 64:8 | I am His workmanship. |
| JEREMIAH 1:5 | He knows me. |
| JEREMIAH 14:9 | I bear His name. |
| JEREMIAH 31:3 | He loves me with an everlasting love. |
| HOSEA 2:14 | He speaks tenderly to me. |
| ZECHARIAH 3:4 | He dresses me in rich garments. |
| MARK 6:31 | He takes me to a quiet place and gives me rest. |
| LUKE 12:33 | He gives me treasure in heaven. |
| JOHN 7:24 | He does not judge me by appearances. |
| JOHN 8:36 | He sets me free. |
| JOHN 15:19 | I am chosen. |
| ROMANS 6:22 | I reap holiness and eternal life. |
| ROMANS 15:7 | I am accepted in the Beloved. |
| 2 CORINTHIANS 2:14 | He makes me the fragrance of life. |
| 2 CORINTHIANS 3:16 | He sees me as I am. |
| 2 CORINTHIANS 4:17 | He turns my hardship to glory. |
| GALATIANS 3:27 | He clothes me with Himself. |
| GALATIANS 5:1 | He delivers me. |
| EPHESIANS 1:3 | He blesses me with every spiritual blessing. |
| EPHESIANS 1:18 | He gives me the riches of His inheritance. |
| EPHESIANS 1:19 | He gives me power. |
| PHILIPPIANS 3:13 | He redeems my past. |
| COLOSSIANS 2:7 | He fills me with thankfulness. |
| 2 THESSALONIANS 2:16 | He gives me hope. |
| 2 THESSALONIANS 2:17 | He encourages my heart. |
| HEBREWS 4:15 | He sympathizes with my weaknesses. |
| 2 PETER 1:3 | He gives me everything I need. |

# I INVITE YOU TO VISIT...

Thank you for letting me share my life with you. I hope this book has touched you in some way and shown you how very special you are. I've told you a lot about myself in these pages; now I'd love to hear from you.

I invite you to visit my Web site and tell me a little about yourself. Has this book given you a greater awareness of your inner beauty and true identity? If so, I'd love to hear about it! During your visit, you can also read more about what I'm doing and be able to contact me about speaking engagements and retreats.

I look forward to meeting you one day soon. Until then, remember: The King is enthralled by your beauty!

Your friend,

*Nancy*

www.nancystafford.com

# NOTES

1. C. S. Lewis, "The Weight of Glory," *The Weight of Glory and Other Addresses* (New York: Macmillan, 1980), 6–7.

2. Ibid., 15–6.

3. Ibid., 18–9.

4. John Trent, *Lifemapping* (Colorado Springs, Colo.: Focus on the Family Publishing, 1994), 16.

5. Serita Ann Jakes, *The Princess Within: Restoring the Soul of a Woman* (Tulsa, Okla.: Albury Publishing, 1999), 63.

6. Brent Curtis and John Eldredge, *The Sacred Romance* (Nashville, Tenn.: Thomas Nelson Publishers, 1997), 88–9.

7. Frederick Buechner, cited in Ibid., 84–5.

8. John and Paula Sandford, *Healing the Wounded Spirit* (Tulsa, Okla.: Victory House, 1985), 62.

9. Sue Monk Kidd, *When the Heart Waits* (San Francisco: HarperSanFransisco, 1990), 59.

10. Dr. Kevin Leman, *When Your Best Is Not Good Enough: The Secret of Measuring Up* (Grand Rapids, Mich.: Flemming H. Revell, 1997), 88.

11. Dr. Nathaniel Branden, *How to Raise Your Self-Esteem* (New York: Bantam Books, 1987), 22–3.

12. Simon Tugwell, quoted in Curtis and Eldredge, 81.

13. Brennan Manning, quoted in Holly Halverson, "Mystics in Our Midst," *Aspire*, December 1997/January 1998, 25.

14. Dr. Henry Cloud and Dr. John Townsend, *Safe People* (Grand Rapids, Mich.: Zondervan Publishing House, 1995), 157.

15. Brennan Manning, quoted in Halverson, 25.

16. Lucille Clifton, "Two-Headed Woman," in Rosalie Maggio, *The New Beacon Book of Quotations by Women* (Boston: Beacon Press, 1996), 75.

17. Isabel Burton, quoted in Maggio, 172.

18. Anne Morrow Lindbergh, *Gift from the Sea* (New York: Pantheon Books, 1950), 50–1.

19. Richard J. Foster, *Celebration of Discipline* (San Francisco: Harper & Row, 1978), 85.

20. Thomas Merton, *The Sign of Jonas* (New York: Harcourt, Brace & Co., 1953), 261.

21. Dallas Willard, *The Spirit of the Disciplines* (San Francisco: HarperCollins, 1988), 160–1.

22. Oswald Chambers, *My Utmost For His Highest* (New York: Dodd, Mead & Company, 1935), 95.

23. Martha Graham, quoted in Maggio, 50.

24. Philip Yancey, *What's So Amazing About Grace?* (Grand Rapids, Mich.: Zondervan Publishing House, 1997), 70.

25. C. S. Lewis, *Reflections on the Psalms* (New York: Harcourt, Brace & World, 1958), 96–7.

Multnomah Publishers®

The publisher and author would love to hear your comments about this book. *Please contact us at:* www.multnomah.net/beautybythebook